柔道家

# The Judoka

by
W. D. Norwood Jr.

# Reviews for the 1st edition

"This extraordinary little novella is reminiscent of Castaneda but far more intelligible."
-Alan Watts

"His direct writing about judo is clear and quietly restrained, hard to match in the literature of the subject."
-New York Times

"The novella reads well without the commentaries and this reader skipped ahead to pick up the story. The commentaries are however well worth the wait if you can."
-Ryan Petty, Austin American-Statesman

"The reader interested in writing or reading poetry, those interested in the art of judo, or those who just simply want to read a fascinating book will enjoy reading The Judoka."
-Pat Grierson, Hattiesburg American

" . . . a beautifully descriptive, beautifully conceived book that should be around for some time to come."
-L. Hart, Los Angeles Free Press

First edition published in the USA by Alfred A. Knopf 1973

This edition is published in the UK and USA
by Masterworks International Publishing
on behalf of
the estate of W. D. Norwood Jr.

Copyright: 1973, 2015

MASTERWORKS INTERNATIONAL
27 Old Gloucester Street
London
WC1N 3XX
UK


Email: admin@mwipublishing.com
Web: http:/www.mwipublishing.com

ISBN: 978-0-9927706-8-6

Cover artwork and Japanese Kanji by Michael Nolan © 2014
(artwork available for purchase at thejudoka.com)

The epigraph by Lao-Tzu is taken from The Way of life According to
Lao-Tzu translated by Witter Bynner, and is reprinted by permission
of G. P. Putnam's Sons. Copyright © 1964 by Witter Bynner

# The Judoka by W. D. Norwood Jr.

## Contents

# Introduction to the New Edition
by
William D. "Dub" Norwood, III

The term "judoka" refers to one who does judo, the modern martial art with origins in 19th century Japan, a fighting art with a particular emphasis on the use of an opponent's own strengths to effect his defeat. The book before you is an account of the adventures of such a man, a judoka, but it is not just about this man, or the martial art he practices. Rather, it is about the "way" of judo, as both a fighting art and an approach to living ("a way"), and what this way might be able to tell us about who we are and who we might choose to become. The book does not prescribe "a way" for others to follow; that is, it does not simply offer advice about what to believe or how to behave, or point out the faults in other ways of being. It simply describes the way of one particular man, with commentary explaining, or rather reasoning through, the choices he has made, with the story presenting the consequences that these choices have for him. The implication, of course, may be that others might also choose to adopt a similar way, having been influenced by the reasoning of the judoka and the consequences that follow from his choices, but I think that the point is rather to draw a portrait of a man in the process of making himself, thorough his art and his actions, and by means of this portrayal to provide a model of self-exploration for others, and a method for finding one's own way amongst the various choices available, some more and some less effective, to give meaning and vitality to action. This novel grew out of an essay published in the Southern Quarterly in 1971 entitled "Judo as Poetic Way." Although judo may be particularly apt as a guide for how one might live "poetically," incorporating as it does values that may be especially useful in negotiating the challenges that life brings, it is here used primarily as an example, a physical and psychological and spiritual metaphor, for a poetic way of being. As the author puts it, "judo as a fighting art is...a way of loving the adversary and of expressing that love in an ironic and aesthetically satisfying matter; thus, it is a poetic method of fighting." This book is an elaboration on that poetic method, and how that method might be generalized more broadly. The reader new to Judo will learn a fair amount about it by reading this book; but even one intimately familiar with this fighting art will likely gain a fresh understanding of its principles, and the implications of those principles for developing a more creative, meaningful, and effective life. As one would expect, from its focus on Judo, the book explores a number of ideas that are likely to be familiar to students of the Eastern religious traditions, particularly Zen Buddhism, but the book is equally concerned with ideas and values in the Western tradition that speak to a Western audience.

The Judoka was originally published in 1973. Bill Norwood, my father, was at that time Chairman of English at the University of Southern Mississippi, in Hattiesburg, what was then a relatively small, southern college town still insulated from many of the cultural changes that were in motion and about to so greatly alter the entire country. Our stay in Mississippi was not to last long, as his own values and those to which the university still clung were just too far apart, but among my most vivid memories of our time in Mississippi are of him sitting in a folding lounge chair in our back yard, under a large fig tree bearing fruit, writing this book on long, yellow, legal pads. His cursive writing was neat and consistent, but illegible to anyone but himself, so periodically he transcribed his notes into type on an ancient Royal typewriter that appeared to be far older than he was. This manual typewriter took force to operate, and the "clack" "clack" "clack" reverberated throughout the house in a staccato rhythm that even now, should I hear something similar, brings to mind a flood of pleasant memories. Although he eventually moved on to a computer and learned to appreciate its advantages, I know he missed his manual typewriter, and the discipline composing on it demanded. I remember him retyping whole pages after changing a single word, which motivated him to craft each sentence carefully before committing it to type. I also vividly remember his common habit, usually very early in the morning but not unusual at other times of the day, of squatting as if about to catch a baseball, with a cup of hot black coffee in one hand and a cigarette in the other (a habit he later let go in the way described in this book) – surveying the barn and the fruit trees behind our house, with the tops of the higher buildings on the university's campus in the distance, with a calm and contemplative demeanor, and a laconic smile. He might squat like that for an hour at a time. As a child of about eight, I would watch this daily ritual and occasionally follow him out there, to the edge of the back patio, and mimic his posture to the best of my ability, teetering over more times than not. My presence was encouraged, but only if I maintained the spirit of the moment by remaining silent, acting as if I knew what he was getting at when he occasionally posed, abstractedly, what were obviously rhetorical questions such as, "Do you notice the wind as it brushes against your skin?" (usually on a windless day) or offered comments quite cryptic for an eight year old, such as, "I think the figs smell riper today." It took me quite a few years to make sense of what we were up to, but eventually it did come into focus. At eight, nine, ten, I was not reading The Judoka, so I didn't yet have access to a summary account of the ideas he was contemplating, or understand how these moments might be interpreted in that framework, but I was absorbing it piecemeal, in snippets of conversations, some directly with him, in language a child could understand, some over-heard in conversations only very minimally understood, and some by living it as he, for example, experimented with the use of massage as an adjunctive treatment for all manner of minor childhood illnesses, or laughed and refused mosquito repellant with the exhortation that loving the mosquito was a far more effective solution to the mosquito "problem" than trying to drive them off with repellant. As I got older, I began to put some of the pieces of this puzzling behavior together, and to make sense of it. I have long since forgotten what thoughts passed through my mind while I was squatting with him on the back patio, but I have forever remembered the ritual. The allotting of time each day to focus awareness on the details of that moment, to survey and get to know the sensations of the body, and to observe and then play with the chatter inside the head. To watch the mind at play by having thoughts, or more importantly, simply allowing the thoughts to have you. Or, at times, letting the thoughts "bubble off" (as he might say) until only aware of awareness itself. I've come to understand this behavior, of course, as a practice of mindfulness, but what strikes me now is not so much that he practiced and reaped the benefits of mindfulness, but the particular way that he chose to share his appreciation for this activity. Rather than tell you something, or attempt to explain it, he would exemplify it and then offer encouragement as your curiosity led you to a desire to explore further, like Plato nursing ideas from Meno. At the center of his approach are some seemingly paradoxical ideas about how the facilitation of the intellectual growth of others might best be served by first learning to let go of the desire to change them, he lived this way with remarkable consistency, and his students (and his children) flourished. He never lived on a beach in a make-shift shelter, but he did often "abandon the social structure built around oneself which supports the old consciousness," (p.132) and in many other ways he sought to live by the principles that guide the judoka in this book.

As I've noted, I've been exposed to the ideas explored in this book since childhood, and they have had a profound effect on my life. Of course, it is not unusual for parents to profoundly influence their children. I am sure that is the very hope that most parents harbor when they contemplate their children's development. I do not mean to suggest that I have been more influenced by my father than others have been by theirs, but I do find myself in the unusual position of being able to able to look back at a work written during my childhood and see a map of many of the ideas that have continued to shape and enrich all aspects of my life. Although I never mastered judo as a martial art, I can say that the principles that inform the practice of judo, as least insofar as they are illustrated in this book, have served me well both personally and professionally, and I find it hard to image what my life might have been like had I never been exposed to these ideas.

As a young child I was a rather robust and healthy child, with but a few anomalous portents of health problems to come. And, indeed, in late adolescence, not long after an undefeated season as an offensive lineman on a suburban high school football team, I was diagnosed with a life-threatening cancer of the lymph system. A disease I have continued to struggle with, in various forms, for the past thirty five years. In that time, I have experienced a wide variety of medical treatments, including thoracic and orbital surgery, radiation, chemotherapy, photopheresis, and bone marrow transplantation, and as a result I have gained a considerable appreciation for the benefits of scientific medicine. But also during many of the years I have grappled with this disease and, sometimes more challenging, the debilitating effects of its treatment, I had my father by my side, modeling the wisdom I was exposed to in childhood, and that you will find in this volume, and in so doing helping me to cultivate vitality in the most unlikely of places, often in a bed in an exceedingly large cancer hospital in Houston, Texas, fully expecting to die. He offered – or rather practiced in front of me – bits of the wisdom he offers in this book, and while the physicians worked on my body, I tried to emulate his very unconventional "way" of being, doing, making, and let go of the pull to focus exclusively on being something I was not (e.g., healthy), finding instead that there is indeed as much life in a moment of pain as there is in a moment of joy. Now I have no way of knowing what role, if any, this way of being with my illness contributed to my survival, or to my subsequent ability to go on to live a full and rewarding life (though often punctuated with periods of illness), it may have played absolutely no role, but I do know that while my peers were determined to "fight" their disease, to struggle against the limitations its treatment imposed, as we are so often encouraged to do by our culture, I chose to take a different stance, and now eighteen years after my transplant, I am the only one of the ten in my cohort, to my knowledge, who remains alive. Even if this approach had no measurable effect on the growth of the disease of my body, or on the effectiveness of the medical treatments I received, I do very much believe without question that it gave me peace when faced with death and helped me find vitality even in the midst of considerable physical suffering.

The ideas presented in this volume have also informed and enriched my professional life. After earning an undergraduate degree in humanities (classical languages and philosophy) and a PhD in clinical psychology, I have spent much of my professional life investigating and teaching empirically-supported therapeutic approaches to the alleviation of psychological suffering, and I have found many of the ideas developed in this book to be exceedingly useful in the practice of psychotherapy and in the training of psychotherapists. Indeed, some of the principles explored in this book, particularly the "wisdom of the East" as the original book jacket puts it, have since become a major focus of scientific interest within academic psychology, and evidence supporting the therapeutic benefits of engaging these psychological processes is now well established. It is clear that my father was prescient in his appreciation for the usefulness of some of the processes central to contemporary approaches to psychotherapy, not only as a means to alleviate psychological suffering but as a way to promote living with purpose and engaging the world with greater effectiveness and vitality. His sophisticated reasoning about language, psychology, epistemology, and philosophy of science remain consistent with much of contemporary theory, forty years later, and in recent years it has been delightful to see so many of these ideas garner the increased scientific scrutiny they deserve. Although the "wisdom of the East" has entered our culture in a variety of ways, and may be quite familiar to some readers, my father's penetrating originality and graceful and insightful interpretation and extension of these ideas will very likely surprise and delight even someone quite familiar with Judo, eastern philosophy, and mindlessness and acceptance processes as they are practiced in the martial arts or applied in contemporary psychology.

I'd also like to make one, more personal, remark. My father and I were close. We shared a number of interests and were fortunate enough to have had the opportunity to recognize and exploit that fact. For the last ten years of his life, except for a year or so when I was completing a clinical forensic internship in North Carolina, we had the habit of meeting every Saturday morning for breakfast or coffee, as early as I could make myself get up. We'd hang around a coffee shop for a couple of hours, talking or debating or just thinking out loud, and then we'd drift off to a bookstore, often more than one, in order to browse before returning to our regular schedules. My father was an avid conversationalist. He loved to talk but he was very willing to listen. And you always felt that you were heard. I know I can speak for my siblings when I say that it has been an enormous gift to have had a father so loving, compassionate, open, and accessible. He had the peculiar habit of looking beyond people's weaknesses and seeing only their strengths. He seems to have had the singular good fortune to have known many, many people who were, as he used to say, "probably the best" at what they did. He extended this praise to his children. Although, I have to admit that we all might have starved as infants had it not been for a practical and loving mother, one whose concerns extended to such things as food, shelter, and clothing; but as a father of grown children, he was wonderful. One really could not have asked for more.

I recall once as a child trying to explain to a schoolmate what my father did for a living. Having been asked, I was startled to see the puzzled look I got in response to my rather matter-of-fact explanation that, "He sits under the fig tree and thinks." That didn't seem to be a very satisfactory answer to my friend, but in retrospect, I think it captured the situation quite accurately. That is, in fact, precisely what he did. He sat, he thought, he read, he wrote, and he talked to people about the things he thought. And sometimes they listened, and their lives were changed. That seems to me to be a particularly admirable job. He has left a legacy that has influenced a great many lives, and it is my hope, will continue to influence those who come to his work through this book.

Homer was wrong in saying: "Would that strife might perish from among gods and men!" He did not see that he was praying for the destruction of the universe; for, if his prayer were heard, all things would pass away
—Heraclitus

But as long as there be a foe, value him,
Respect him, measure him, be humble toward him;
Let him not strip from you, however strong he be,
Compassion, the one wealth which can afford him.
—Lao Tzu

# The Judoka

# 戦 FIGHTING

The Judoka walks along the beach almost wholly absorbed in the saltsea-and-fish smell and the water-glass clarity of the waves over the white sand. It is late afternoon. He is wearing only a pair of Levis and would get rid of those were there no other people in sight. But there are other people in sight: a young woman in a yellow bathing suit walking a hundred yards ahead of him, and beyond her four men approaching.

When the four men reach the young woman, they stop her. One of them takes her arm and starts to pull her, but she resists and frees herself. Another reaches out and toys with her long black hair. It becomes apparent that the teasing is not friendly and that the woman is in trouble. The Judoka notes irritably the impending disturbance of his walk, but the mood passes quickly. The woman looks around, sees the Judoka, and runs toward him, calling for help. The men—hardly more than boys, really, but strong and cocky—walk after her, not rushing at all.

As the men get closer, the Judoka imagines the whole scene as if he were a spectator. Inwardly, he laughs at himself: he doesn't really like adventure, at least not in the moments before a crisis.

He feels fear even as he nods acceptance of the woman's appeal, feels it despite his opinion that the four-headed, eight-armed monster playing dragon to his St. George is unlikely to fight at all and that, even if it does, some of the heads and arms will be inactive or ineffectual or even in the way. The men keep coming, more slowly now, two of them grinning cruelly. The fear grows. The Judoka makes no attempt to block it. Now he trembles and feels a sinking of the stomach, a touch of nausea, but also a surge of strength. The beach, enchanted a few minutes before, now seems sordid.

One of the men, the redheaded one, tells him that he had better get out of the way. He would like to, but across his mind's eye flickers a picture of himself running and the young woman with long black hair watching him, and the image triggers a counterfear and stabilizes him. He stands still. The men too are now standing still, a few feet from him. Deliberately he wipes from his mind the image of himself and the woman in the yellow bathing suit. He focuses all his attention on his opponents, seeing in their faces fear much like his own but mixed with anger. He feels with their anger and in so doing grows an anger of his own. These men are going to hurt him, and he them; they are going to plunge into and destroy him, and he is going to penetrate and destroy them. So be it. He feels almost a lust for union in combat.

The redhaired man bends and picks up a heavy piece of driftwood. The Judoka wonders idly if he will actually attack. Suddenly he does.

He slashes with the stick at the Judoka's head, but the Judoka has stepped inside the arc of the stick and twisted away from it. The other three men cannot yet figure out how to get into the fight;

they are motionless. The young woman wants to help her defender, but, like most people to whom combative contact is unfamiliar, she is unable to move in the moment of crisis. The Judoka throws his hip into the redhead's midsection and clamps an arm around his neck. In a second movement so swift and smooth it seems a continuation of the first, the Judoka swings his leg hard against the redhead's legs. The stick is still following its original path, but now the redhead is following it, his feet high in the air. In turn, the Judoka is following him.

The Judoka is now caught up in an ecstasy of crisis. He is fully aware of the beauty in the developing pattern, but he does not let the pattern take over fully and control the situation: he continues to play as well as be played. As he falls, he is deciding whether or not to let his body crush his adversary's chest against the ground. He decides that he must hit hard, and he does so, although not quite so hard as he might. The redhead is stunned.

But now another man, a tall and sinewy one, dives at the Judoka and pins him to the ground. He strikes with his left fist at the Judoka's face, but the Judoka turns his face with the blow, and the fist only skins his cheek in passing. The Judoka grabs the wrist as it goes by in his left hand and pulls it in the direction it is already going. Suddenly the tall man is on his back on top of the Judoka. As the tall man tries to turn over, the Judoka, still holding the wrist, grips the elbow in his right hand and pushes. The tall man screams. The Judoka relaxes the pressure for an instant and then drives it home, breaking the arm and simultaneously throwing the tall man off to the side.

In almost the same motion the Judoka regains his feet and faces the two men remaining. But they hesitate, and now their opportunity is lost. One asks timidly if he can help the stunned redhead.

"Certainly," the Judoka replies.

For several seconds the young woman has been fascinated by what she thinks of as the Judoka's "savage grace." Now she observes with surprise that his face shows no contempt for the two men who do not fight; his expression is almost tender.

As he turns away, the young woman steps up to him and touches his bleeding cheek, but he smiles and says that he will dash saltwater on it. She sees that he is completely spent.

A little later he walks her back to town.

単戈

Judo is more than a fighting art. Like the other Oriental martial arts, it is a *way* in the Oriental sense: a way of doing anything and of simply being. The fighting method is just its focus.

Any art is a way of doing something. Its principles can be applied to other activities. When the principles of an art are applied to a person's general behavior, the method of that art becomes for that person a way.

Living an art as Way clearly affects the practice of the art. With judo, it is easy to see how this works. The essence of judo is a peculiar response to an adversary's moves—to push when pulled, pull when pushed. Obviously a person who responds to people and events literally and figuratively in this manner has an advantage in all that he does—albeit a split second advantage—over a person who does not; that is, he does in a judo contest or situation. It is likely that most masters of all arts practice their arts as aspects of ways, even though they do not use those terms.

But it is equally clear that it would be foolish for any person to adopt a life style merely to master an art—unless the way, the life style, is of value for its own sake; in which case, the highest function of the art is to train and focus the life style.

Judo is a poetic way. It has critical value for Westerners for precisely the same reason that it is usually misunderstood in the West. Our culture fragments things—as it has broken judo the fighting art from judo the life style—and many of its ills result from fragmentation. Judo, like Zen, from which it derives, and like poetry, unifies.

The situation of hand-to-hand combat is worthy of the attention of anyone, male or female, young or old, for it is a rather good microcosm of the general human situation. In it, a person's mind and spirit are as fully involved as his body. A human relationship is at work. Social and moral and even economic factors influence what happens. Stance on the earth and relation to the air affect the outcome. The judo approach to that microcosm, then, has metaphoric significance. My own belief is that judo constitutes a valuable *working metaphor*: one by which a person can learn to cope with events and within which he can operate in the events.

A *judoka* is one who practices judo. The Judoka of my sketch is perhaps not quite a master, but he is at least on the path to mastery, and he practices judo as Way. We see him first in a rather ordinary activity, walking along a beach.

When we first meet him, his mind is blank. It isn't quite still, for it registers the rhythmic sound of the waves, the people in the environment, and so on; but it seems to have a kind of stillness at its core. It is empty of concepts, and it is empty of images other than those presently transmitted by his senses. This is not because the Judoka is lazy, lacks imagination, or cannot handle concepts. Many masters of the martial arts practice, in meditation, letting thought "bubble off" and the mind grow blank as a way of developing the acuteness of perception they desire, a kind of sixth sense. The Judoka has done this in the past, but he is not now doing it as an exercise. He is doing what the exercise attempts to train one to do—to live in the present, the here and now, the non-verbal world of pure experience. He is completely abandoned to his present activity, almost like a child, without concern for what he must do later in the day. (If he should want to think about something he would do so; he is *letting* himself be, not forcing himself to be, in this state of mind.) He is doing this just because it is pleasant. Abandonment to the moment, especially when it takes the form of absorption in nature, tends to lend enchantment to the world. The abstract concerns of the mind sometimes tend to dissipate that enchantment. When one gets beyond these abstract concerns, the world may look again rather as it does to a child.

Perhaps the ability to enter this state of mind at will can be developed only by those people who have sufficient confidence in their environment to free themselves of bondage to the economic system and sufficient faith in themselves to do what they want to do all of the time. At first thought, this seems an impossible set of conditions, but in practice it amounts to little more than developing a preference for walking over riding and learning that, for instance, judo can be practiced without a gi (the heavy jacket and loose pants modeled after the Oriental peasant costume that people associate with the sport) and outside a *dojo* (training hall with mats).

When the trouble starts in front of the Judoka, he feels discomfort because he knows that his walk is going to be interrupted and he is thoroughly enjoying his walk. Then his habitual way of regarding the world asserts itself and affects him as I am affected by G. K. Chesterton's remark that inconvenience properly regarded is adventure, whereas adventure improperly regarded is inconvenience; consequently, his mood passes. To be in an adventure is to feel with Clappique (in André Malraux's *Man's Fate*) that "now I am in a story." This feeling, too, lends enchantment to the world. However, it is a feeling that may fade somewhat under the shadow of fear.

At first the Judoka does not feel fear: he is detached, viewing the scene as a spectator. Detachment is the virtue of saints, but it is not quite what it is sometimes taken to be, a complete absence of desire or fear. It is absence of desire for particular things so great as to make one grasp after them, or absence of fear of particular things so great as to make one avoid them at all costs. It is, then, an acceptance of the world as it is, an acceptance of what is offered. It is an essential quality for judo. While the Judoka's sense of detachment is temporarily weakened by his fear, he retains the basic quality.

*De*tachment from particular things is the obverse side of *at*tachment to all things, to the process of life itself. If one is attached to the whole, or what is beyond the whole, or the process, or God-whatever the words—one has faith, and thus need not be attached to any particular thing. To be attached to any particular thing, to *have* to have it or *have* to avoid it, is to idolize it. To idolize anything is to blow it up out of proportion, to distort it, to create an illusion, a superstition, and therefore to behave in a fashion that simply does not work. The most common of idols is the ego, that illusory picture of the self that a person carries in his mind's eye and defends against all comers, often to his own loss. Ordinarily, when a person rids himself of this idol he automatically rids himself of all others, and he becomes detached.

A person reared in the United States finds it difficult to accept the world as it is, for he or she has been taught to believe in progress, i.e., precisely non-acceptance of the world, improvement of it. But the world is not to be improved, nor is anything in it to be improved. (I realize that this raises a question as to why I write this book, or you read it, or anyone practices judo.) The world is like a seesaw: one end has to go down when the other end goes up. There is no raising of the fulcrum, or very little. (I must leave that "very little" as leeway, for the doctrine I am enunciating is, like all other doctrines, at once true, and false.) To accept the world as it is is to see the world as good by definition (as whichever side of me the earth is on is *down* by definition), and to accept and even delight in whatever the world offers without having to grasp after anything or attempt to hold on to anything or to dread anything.

Curiously, it is only the person who is detached who can really *appreciate* the world as one appreciates poetry—experiences it in its true nature, is immersed in it, gains a heightened consciousness by means of it. Curiously too, the person who does not grasp is more likely to get the prize than the one who does.

Detachment is a necessary quality for the Judoka for many reasons. One is that his art demands his acceptance of what his adversary offers. Another is that if the idea of winning, for instance, is idolized, attention is diverted from the adversary. Another is that if the ego is idolized, the judoman is too defensive and rigid or too aggressive and careless to be effective. Another is that if he blocks off—refuses to accept—fear or anger, he fails to use it to his advantage, and he suffers thereby.

The Judoka accepts fear as he does everything else. It has its uses: readying one's body for sudden movement, alerting one to possible dangers in the environment, and calling attention to likely strengths of the enemy. These functions are valuable in that a fight is likely to take place when one is neither physically nor mentally ready for such an occurrence, amid furniture or railings or other obstacles, and between people who do not know each other especially well.

So far in this book, I have used the words *mind* and *body* or *mental* and *physical*, as if they really refer to different things.

I do not think they do. I think them merely linguistic conveniences—now grown into superstitions—for enabling us to discuss various aspects of what is in fact a mind-body, a person, in whom the component aspects work as a unit. In other words, where the mind goes, there the body is also, and vice versa. The fear that readies the body for battle thereby also readies the mind.

The readying process is not necessarily a pleasant one. C. S. Lewis writes that the trouble with lust is that it disenchants the universe; fear and anger seem to me to do the same thing. But this disenchantment or unpleasantness has a function also: a person can perhaps abandon his ego if the world is evil or ugly enough. (Perhaps the reason one has to suffer before reaching enlightenment is that one can get rid of excessive concern for self only in the dark night of the soul). When the self-image wants no protection, fear is gone, for fear results from imagining future damage to that image.

Thus, given time, fear welcomed could do its own work and then dispose of itself. Since he has little time, the Judoka speeds the process by arousing a counterfear and deliberately wiping his self-image from his mind. But his central act is to let the fear run, without blocking it. The reader who knows judo will recognize that this welcoming of a force besetting oneself is itself a form of judo.

The Judoka's next act, focusing attention and specifically *sympathetic* attention on the adversary, is necessary. It is also fairly difficult to do. Sympathetic attention comes close to being a definition of *love*. What the Judoka does is to love his enemy.

This love of the adversary is essential to good judo. One who can learn to love his opponent—to pay close and sympathetic attention to him, to help him express himself and do what he desires to do—and who contests for love of the game, rather than in the hope of winning something, can be a successful judoman. This is not merely a mouthing of an old sports cliché: it is a specific and demonstrable statement about the mind-set (which is also the body-set) that is conducive to good judo. A person who loves his adversary concentrates his attention on the adversary rather than on himself: thus he effectively submerges or loses his ego. The key to effective judo as all texts agree is ability to sense the opponent's *kuzushi*; that is, his balance or lack of it. This sensing of kuzushi is a fine and subtle art requiring very close attention to the actual opponent and what he is actually doing. In different ways, indifference and hatred distort one's image of the opponent; accurate, fine sensing is possible only in love. Finally, to push when pulled, pull when pushed, is precisely to let the adversary express himself—indeed, to *help* him to express himself. To understand what he wants to express and to feel with that expression and assist it is to sympathize; that is, to love. Indifference ignores the expression; hatred rejects it.

But it is not easy to love an adversary, especially under conditions usual to a fight. In this instance, the Judoka does it by noting that these men probably share with him a common experience of fear (although they are probably blocking theirs). In that he and they are partaking of the same experience, he and they are seeing the world through glasses with similar lenses. They are the same kind of animal. To feel this is to feel union; that is to say, love. Feeling sympathy in one matter, the Judoka has no trouble feeling it in others.

The first new sympathy the Judoka feels is especially valuable to him. His opponents are angry, so he, sympathetically, grows angry. But his anger is not, like theirs, directed at himself—he has no cause to be angry at himself—so he directs his at them. He does have cause to be angry at them. Whereas fear readies the person for either flight or battle, anger readies him specifically for battle. Wisely, the Judoka welcomes the anger just as he did the fear, yielding to his own emotions just as he does to the enemy.

Prepared now, the Judoka feels a thrill of impending conflict, a kind of love of battle. A man who accepts the world as it is and delights in it loves strife, for there can be no love without strife, any more than there can be hope without fear or detachment without attachment. The detached and enlightened man delights in both poles. The Judoka, realizing that he is about to enter an act of love, naturally feels something like desire. It is the other pole of his fear.

Now we come to the combat itself and see judo as fighting art. The *ju* in *judo* is usually translated as "gentle." The whole term judo, then, is read as "gentle way." The translation can be misleading, although it is not necessarily incorrect: anyone who has seen *shiai* (a match) knows that judo is at times more like a high wind than a "gentle" breeze. There is an older sense of "gentle" that approaches "noble," and, so understood, the translation works but is not very helpful. One can best understand judo as "gentle way," perhaps, by taking "gentle" to mean "loving"—but also remembering that love is sometimes violent.

To say that judo is a "way of the lover" is to suggest a paradox. The paradox or apparent breakdown in the analogy between loving and fighting arises when one considers the incompatibility of aim in conflict. Lovers seem to have a common goal, fighters opposite ones. But this opposition is more apparent than real. It would seem that what an adversary really wants is to defeat you, and that if you really want to help him you will simply give up and let him win. But this seeming is incorrect.

Without conflict there can be no story. Or, to say the same thing another way, life itself *is* contest or conflict. (The word "is" sets up an equation. I am not saying that life should contain conflict; I am saying that life equates to conflict, that life and conflict are synonymous). Insofar as any person is fully alive, or even desires to come fully alive, what he or she really wants—his True Self, not necessarily his conscious ego—is conflict, not victory that concludes conflict. The desire for victory is in part the natural motive for conflict and in part merely a superficial desire of the conscious ego for its own gratification. Insofar as it is the latter, *it never fully controls the person*; the desires of the True Self do that, although they may be impeded by the self-division caused by the conscious ego's working at cross-purposes. What your adversary really wants, therefore, is not for you to give up, but for you to make a good fight of it.

If a good fight or contest goes on long enough, one person or the other tires of it and actually desires the conflict to end, regardless of who is victor. Clearly, at this point, he can make it end more readily by losing than by winning. This is exactly what happens in most close judo matches, even though he who loses may never admit to himself consciously that he has chosen to lose.

It is important to note that the difference in the contestants is the degree of life in them and that the end of the fight is implicit in its beginning. (These conditions do not absolve anyone of responsibility for his own actions, since the exercise of responsibility is also a function of life or True Self. It should be noted that I use the terms *life* and *True Self* as synonymous). The duty of both contestants or fighters—to life or True Self or God, which is to say to themselves and to each other——is the same: to fight well and let the outcome unfold of itself. This permitting to unfold may be accomplished in a spirit of love, even if the unfolding entails a man's death. But only *permitting*; no forcing of events may be accomplished in a spirit of love, and any forcing of events that results in death or injury is absolutely immoral. (It is immoral even if it does not result in death or injury, but the immorality is perhaps not so obviously serious.)

I realize that this doctrine is dangerous if followed by any but honest and able men. But so, I think, is any doctrine. I write it because it must be understood if the concept of judo as loving way is to make any sense.

A definition of judo that is more immediately helpful than "gentle way" is "yielding way." Yielding is pulling when pushed, helping the adversary to achieve what he desires. The Judoka operates somewhat in the manner of an unlatched door when someone who expects it to be latched crashes into it with his shoulder. Jigaro Kano, the man who in the late nineteenth century devised judo out of the remnants of the dying Samurai fighting art of *ju-jitsu*, described the yielding device in this way: Suppose two men are struggling by pushing against each other. One has a strength of ten units, the other of seven. If they continue to push directly against each other, the ten-unit man will inevitably overcome his opponent. But if the seven-unit man suddenly reverses his effort with, say, three of his units, all the effort is going one way—and the seven-unit man has four units left with which to direct the flow of the movement. All judo throws are based on this device; so judo can be accurately described as a "yielding way."

But the phrase does not quite wholly describe judo. In the first place, there are aspects of judo, notably choking and striking (the latter used in combative but not competitive judo), that are not at all based on the yielding principle. In the second place, in no judo is the yielding principle complete: to yield completely would be simply to surrender. The yielding in judo is a tempered or controlled submission.

It seems to me that the most helpful definition of judo is "poetic way." Poetry includes both love and yielding in that the poet can write successfully only about what he loves and to which he therefore yields; he is a true poet only when he merges for a moment with his subject, yet maintains even in the merger a degree of separation from it. The word "poetry" is more specific than "love" and more adequate to explain judo than "yielding." In defining judo as poetic way, I do not mean to assert that it is more poetic than other ways (although I think it more highly poetic than most) but that its defining characteristic is poetry and that, therefore, a true poetic response to any situation will be the "correct" and pragmatically appropriate response in judo.

Poetry is not just verse, although it is traditionally regarded as having its highest expression in that medium. It is of prime importance in our context that we regard as poetry anything—*anything* at all—that has the quality that I shall call *radiance*: the power to arouse an excitement, a new and heightened consciousness, that seems to the person aroused to have positive value and to have a ring of profound truth to human experience.

Technically, poetry derives chiefly from the faculties of synthesis and imagination—the putting-together faculties—as logic or science derives chiefly from those of analysis and abstraction, the taking-apart faculties. Also, poetry is that which judges and is judged by aesthetic response as science judges and is judged by logical validity.

This matter deserves a brief digression for the sake of those readers who have a hearts-and-flowers-and-soft-music concept of poetry. Analysis is the breaking down of things into their component parts, usually for the sake of understanding them. Synthesis is the putting of things together, usually for the sake of using or enjoying them. Abstraction is a form of analysis. It is the taking of qualities out of objects. (No one has ever seen roundness or blue. We abstract the qualities of roundness and blueness from round and blue objects.) Imagination is a form of synthesis, a making of new images by putting together abstractions. The faculties of analysis and abstraction are called "logical," those of synthesis and imagination "poetic." Since the Renaissance, Western culture has come to depend more and more exclusively on the logical—and thus has developed a lack of perspective similar to that of a one-eyed man. The resultant fragmentation is what gives judo as poetic way its special value for the West in our time. Further, poetry judges and is judged by aesthetic response, the quality of human feeling engendered. Logic and science consider aesthetic response irrelevant, except in the special case of logical validity—which is simply one kind of aesthetic response. This narrow concern with human feeling takes a human toll.

James Joyce, following Aquinas, describes poetry as something that is characterized by wholeness, internal harmony, and radiance. Wholeness and interior harmony (a thing is not really whole unless its parts are harmonious with each other and with the whole) are related to synthesis; radiance stimulates and is supported by imagination. Actually, wholeness and radiance are aspects of the same quality, for that which is truly whole has radiance, perhaps because it is a complete pattern and complete patterns excite us and affect consciousness. They excite us perhaps because we recognize in them some kind of truth with relation to nature itself or to the process behind nature. That which is radiant has the kind of wholeness in which we are interested.

It is apparent that whatever is poetic is imaginative. It is not quite so apparent but equally true that whatever is poetic is spontaneous. Planning is largely, though not exclusively, a matter of the intellect and the analytic reason. Spontaneity is a continuous imaginative process, not necessarily confined by logic though deeply reasonable. H. R. F. Keating has a detective story in which one of the characters, a Zen master, explains: "In judo, life has to be lived the Zen way. It insists on action without thought. It casts off the shackles of logic which tells us that a force directed toward one necessarily must strike. A force is only a force: it can go in any direction."

Christmas Humphreys, who calls judo "the Japanese science of defeating one's opponent by his own force," puts the matter this way: "In this form of wrestling the mind must be balanced evenly between aggression and defense. Relaxed yet tense, the body follows a mind whose muscles are equally trained by long development. Unconcerned with thoughts of victory or defeat, or indeed with any thoughts at all, the man of Judo waits for the attack and when it comes answers without thought but with the instantaneous and 'spontaneous' counteract which throws his opponent with the very force with which he moved in to attack."

The interior harmony of judo consists in part of the way in which its throws and grappling methods work back and forth on each other—one serving as a good feint for another, for example—in such ways that the whole of judo is more than the sum of its parts.

The wholeness of judo is most vividly apparent in the use of kuzushi, the way in which judo involves the whole person of both *tori* and *uke* (attacker and attacked) rather than just certain limbs and areas of the body, and in the function of pattern completion.

Kuzushi is the relation of the whole man to the earth upon which he stands. The Judoka never opposes his opponent's kuzushi; on the contrary, he depends upon it for assistance. It would have been worse than useless for him to try to throw the charging redhead backward. The Judoka naturally but quite deliberately threw him forward and slightly to the side—the direction he was going and in which he was off balance. Thus the Judoka used the redhead's kuzushi, exaggerating it to an extreme by sweeping the man's legs out from under him. The Judoka made use of the tall man's kuzushi when the latter swung and missed solid contact: the missed blow carried the tall man across the Judoka's body; the Judoka assisted its effect and thereby turned the man over on his back, where he was at the Judoka's mercy (or, in this particular case, his lack of mercy). In neither instance did the Judoka himself make any attempt to do anything but take advantage of his adversary's relation to the earth.

The Judoka's whole body is his physical weapon. With the redhead he uses his hip to break the charge, his leg to sweep the adversary's feet from beneath him, his arm to lock and twist and direct the head, and the weight of his torso to smash against the chest. The whole body of the redhead is affected. With the tall man, the Judoka uses only his cheek and his two arms, but he turns the tall man's whole body and then breaks the arm. The judo seen in this fight is holistic in that it works by means of or on the whole persons of the participants.

Pattern completion is an aspect of both wholeness and radiance. In both cases in the story, and in most cases in judo generally, the pattern is a circle. The redhead aims his stick in the direction of the ground and then follows it end over end in a kind of giant circle. The tall man's pattern is one that would be indicated diagrammatically by an arrow circling his waist. This O pattern, like its traditional twin the X pattern, is aesthetically satisfying; that is to say, radiant.

X patterns occur in judo also, but are more important in a figurative than in a literal sense. Dramatic irony, the turning of tables, as when the aimed blows of the redhead and the tall man result directly in their own defeat, is a figurative X pattern. Dramatic irony lies at the very heart of judo, for yielding is an ironic process by which accommodation becomes aggression and vice versa.

Radiance, that quality evoking aesthetic response, is determined by what *feels good*, not in a superficial sense, but in a sense of being profoundly pleasing, perhaps in having a ring of deep truth to it. An activity that is aesthetically satisfying is pleasing—albeit perhaps painful—in its means as well as its ends. (By this criterion, natural childbirth may be for the woman an aesthetically satisfying activity; surgery, from the patient's point of view, is not.) When the Judoka pulls the tall man's arm on across his body, he is taking, of the options available to him, the one that feels best—the one that is most pleasing in its means as well as its end.

Probably the chief advantage of defining judo as poetic way is that doing so points up the value of the concept of radiance in determining the proper move at any stage of judo. My own small contribution to judo theory is this: *Whenever a master judoman has options, he will select that one which is most pleasing aesthetically.* In other words, the more truly poetic and especially ironic a person's responses are, the better he will perform judo.

All physical arts including judo are imaginative in an important respect that has been little noted: the images on the mind's eye control in large measure a person's physical activity. Suppose, for example, there is an I-beam twenty feet long and eight inches wide. It is lying on the ground. Someone says to you, "Please walk the length of that I-beam, seeing if you can avoid falling off." You think it absurd even to suggest that you might fall off but you go ahead, and you walk it successfully. But now suppose that the I-beam spans the space between two fourth-floor windows. Now do you want to walk it? Now are you so sure that you will not fall off? And if you do walk it, you are very likely to fall off. What is the difference? The difference is that in the first case you have a mental image—a kind of fictional portrayal—of yourself successfully walking the beam; in the second case you have an image of yourself falling. *And your image will very likely control what you do.* You are hypnotized, one way or the other, by your image. So it is in all physical activities. In judo, a clear notion of oneself as a person who yields, a precise idea of the maneuver one is trying to conduct, and a picture of the adversary in the position in which one hopes to put him are as important as knowledge of technique.

I must hasten to add that while the harboring of detrimental images (winning or losing the fight, being embarrassed, etc.) is always bad for the fighter, the harboring of beneficial ones is good *only* if the images are somewhat to the back of the mind—as the image of a maneuver will be once the technique has been fully mastered—and *only* if the images are allowed to play on the mind's eye screen *only* at the moment of action. The image of a throw held at the front of the mind prior to the instant the adversary is open to that throw—his kuzushi right for it—is very likely to lead one into attempting the throw at an inopportune time. Worse, it is likely to lead one into attempting to force an opportunity to make the throw. This is bad judo, hardly ever successful, and it is the very antithesis of the basic judo attitude of letting things happen as they will. In short, the imagination can be a great aid in judo, but only if properly used. As a weapon, the imagination is a fine instrument, which can be devastating to an opponent but which, mishandled, can be equally devastating to the operator.

The point is that neither images nor conceptual planning should be permitted to interfere with the spontaneity of judo. Spontaneity is an essential poetic quality for good judo. Planned activity works well on material that stands still, and indeed has some value even in dealing with live situations, but some degree of spontaneity is necessary in dealing with a situation susceptible to change and inconsistency.

As the Judoka falls on the redhaired man he is caught up in the ecstasy of the developing pattern set in motion by himself (and the redhaired man). This ecstasy is the other side of the nausea he feels earlier. It is caused in part by the simple excitement of the crisis. But it is also caused in part by the beauty of the pattern: it is the aesthetic response elicited by the pattern. There is a curious relationship between the man and the developing pattern, and this relationship must be understood if one is to understand the spontaneity of judo.

While the Judoka lets things happen as they will, this letting is limited. He accepts the adversary's kuzushi and his attack and responds to them. The adversary responds in turn, and then the Judoka responds to the new situation. The Judoka may initiate an action, but he never *forces* one. In a sense, he lets the situation and the adversary's moves and the pattern that results from mutual responses control his action. *But only in a sense.* In another and equally important sense, the Judoka is always free and is always choosing the most artistic and satisfying move in the light of changing circumstances. In other words, he never tries to let the maneuver in which he is engaged become automatic, to retire from the action and let what he has already set in motion take over. This is an important point, for most of us have a tendency to want to apply some kind of standard technique to a situation and then rest and let the technique take over. The Judoka relaxes as much as possible—his manner is a relaxed and easy one—but he does not rest in the sense of stepping aside. He plays the game all the time. The pattern controls, but the Judoka controls. In the paradox lies the definition of spontaneity. It is a continuous imaginative relationship between the man and his circumstances.

The state of mind conducive to this spontaneity is called by the Zen masters, or rather by those who translate them into English, *no-mind*. The Judoka is in this state of mind when we first see him walking along the beach, then he loses it momentarily but regains it as the fight starts. No-mind is considered the most vital quality to be developed in any practitioner of the martial arts.

Judo as fighting art is a very complicated matter, but it is also a very simple matter in that it is all reducible to a particular attitude or stance in the world—a state of mind and body that can be adopted all at once. Most people cannot hold it for long without considerable practice and, even then, they may often slip; but they can do it briefly, and they can gradually build up the duration of holding. Furthermore, much of the stance is "natural" for many people; more accurately, these people have maintained parts of a whole attitude that is natural for everyone. For that is what the Judoka's attitude is: a childlike attitude tempered by experience and education. Development of that attitude, which is still there for everyone under layers of habit, is a matter of scraping off habit.

戦

It is dusk, and the Judoka is walking along the beach toward town with the young woman in the yellow bathing suit. A few stars are out.

She has expressed her gratitude, and now the two walk side by side in silence, the woman at the edge of the water. The silence is curious to her in that it is very pleasant; ordinarily she has to know a person quite well before she can be with him comfortably in silence. But this man does not seem to expect her to talk, does not seem to feel a responsibility to make conversation himself, yet seems to enjoy the walk and enjoy her presence.

She notices a shell that interests her, and she kneels to inspect it. After a few seconds she remembers that the man is doing her a favor and that she should not inconvenience him further. She glances up at him; he is watching her, half smiling, not showing the least sign of impatience.

"Angel Wing," he says. "A kind of clam."

"Yes," she says, "I know. I study shells."

For several seconds she looks at him, and then she knows that she need neither hurry nor apologize for not hurrying, indeed that he would regard apology as superfluous. For this quality she likes him; it is a quality she has found rare among men.

They walk on, the woman with the flowing black hair carrying the Angel Wing. The Judoka has lapsed again into a state of no-mind, but with his focus now on the woman: her quiet dignity somehow combined with a girlish pleasure in the casual walk, her scent mingled with the salt breeze, the recalled sound of her voice and the present sound of her feet in the sand, the color of the bathing suit, which affects him almost nostalgically. He does nothing with these perceptions; simply takes them in and enjoys them.

As she walks, the young woman takes on the Judoka's mood as if by contagion. She feels a stillness at the center of her being contrasting delightfully with the rhythm of her outer self and of the man and of the waves. She thinks little now, but notices the stars, now bright, and the freshening breeze against her skin. Increasingly she is aware of the man and of his awareness of her and of the kind of atmosphere set up by their mutual presence.

She realizes that she is being bitten by a mosquito. She slaps at it. She looks over at the Judoka, who is regarding her with amusement.

"There's one on you too," she says.

"Let him eat," the Judoka answers. He makes no move to brush it off.

She laughs. Somehow the remark is characteristic of the man. She is surprised, but somehow not surprised. Watching, she notices that very few mosquitoes land on him. That accounts for it, she thinks.

A little farther along the beach he asks her to wait for a minute. He walks up the sand away from the water to a loose clump of bushes. He goes on inside the ring of bushes, and she chuckles, wondering how she could possibly have been curious about what he was going to do. She turns toward the water. But soon he returns wearing a khaki shirt and carrying a pair of sandals. Her surprise shows.

He grins. "That's my apartment," he says.

"You mean you're camping out?"

"Sort of permanently, although not necessarily in this particular spot," he replies.

"I suppose you get to feed a lot of mosquitoes," she says, the challenge softened by a smile.

"Some," he says. "But then the bed is the right firmness, the furniture suits me, the ventilation is good, the ceiling is magnificent, and the rent is low."

The woman starts to comment again about the mosquitoes, but somehow it is difficult to imagine this man being very uncomfortable.

They walk on. She asks what he does, and he says that he is a judo instructor, which is not the whole truth but is the easiest explanation. She recalls seeing his notice posted in the hotel offering lessons to both men and women.

"What do you do?" he asks.

"Well," she says slowly, "I'm a graduate student in English. But my real interest is in interpretive dance, and I pick up a little extra money by coming down to the beach from time to time and collecting shells and driftwood to sell to craft shops back home." She laughs. "That's a more complicated answer than you expected, isn't it?"

"Why this beach?" the Judoka asks. "Is it an especially good hunting ground?"

"No," she says, "but it isn't bad." She explains that she selected this place because of the hotel—it's small, without neon trappings, and with big windows, screened porches, and much old, polished wood. He approves her choice and says so.

The Judoka watches the girl walk and decides that she is no doubt a fine dancer. He looks at her face, which is not quite beautiful but is obviously strong. "If your interest is in dance," he says, "why are you studying English?"

She stops walking and turns to him. "It'll take a few minutes to explain," she says.

"All right," he answers. "There's a log we can sit on."

"It's not that I'm more interested in dance than in literature— I'm interested in both. My mother named me after a girl in one of Yeats's poems that fascinated her. Mother taught me the poem and interpreted it for me when I was quite young, and the poem was pretty rough for a child. Anyway, after I learned the poem and started saying it, I wanted to act it out. The acting out became a dance, and the poem-and-dance combination thrilled me as the poem alone had thrilled my mother. Ever since, that's what I've wanted to do: interpret poems and stories in dance."

"Does that necessitate the formal study of poetry?"

The woman frowns. "You've been around a university yourself," she says.

"Yes," he replies. He offers no further comment.

"There is a great deal to learn about poetry and narrative for the person who wants to handle them well," she says. "Let me explain it this way: First of all, I'm interested in poems and stories themselves. And I'm especially interested in recitation of poems and stories—an art that seems to be dying out. Do you want to hear about that?" She looks sharply at the man, who, whatever his background, is after all a streetfighter, presumably uninterested in poetry. But his face is attentive; if he is putting on an act, it is a very good one.

"I have a theory," she continues, "that a medium which allows play for the imagination has a strength lacking in one that does too much for you—and thus that storytelling, print or voice, can do things that film and television cannot. Once my aunt gave my nephew a play horse for Christmas—one of those plastic ones, realistic in every detail. The little boy next door got a stick horse. For the first two weeks, both boys wanted the plastic horse. Then for the next two months they fought over the stick horse. Do you understand? The stick horse left more room for their imaginations to play . . . That's why I hate to see storytelling and poetry go out of style . . . But who listens to storytellers now, or, except in the hippie coffeehouses, to poetry readers? One has to put on a show with it. Interpretive dance is one way of doing it."

The woman looks into the eyes of the man and sees that he does understand. Both of them recognize in the meeting of their eyes a rapport going beyond verbal understanding.

48

"Who was the girl in the poem?" the Judoka asks.

"Her name was Leda. She was a beautiful woman, and she was raped, but my mother was not certain whether what came of it was good or bad, so she didn't want to quite identify me with her. So she changed the spelling, and I guess the pronunciation, I'm not sure. She called me Leeda."

The Judoka shifts his posture on the log and squats in the manner of a cowboy.

"The dancing," Leeda says, "is an adjunct to the poetry, I guess, or you could say it the other way. I have another theory—"she smiles, "I'm loaded with them. Poetry appeals to the body as well as to the mind. That's why rhythm and meter are important. It's all wrong to sit and read poetry silently. A poem comes alive when it's read aloud and the reader responds to it with his whole person. The interpretive dancer gets to do that. She takes what the poet has done, what he has given, and extends it, carries it through herself and into the world . . . Oh, I can't say what I mean. We'd better be getting on."

The Judoka stands and gives the girl his hand, and as they walk he continues to hold it lightly in his.

"Poetry going through the body," the Judoka says slowly, pondering, "parallels what happens in judo, which is also a matter of something going through both mind and body . . . So does taking what is given and extending it. That's almost a definition of judo."

Leeda looks up, brushing aside her long black hair. "Will you take me as a judo student?" she asks.

"Of course. You can pay me by performing for me."

The young woman laughs. "We'll have to see about that," she says.

By now the stars are very bright. Leeda sees another shell and turns toward the water, stoops and picks it up, and stands looking at it.

The Judoka lets his eyes wander over her back, her legs, and her hips. He feels a small, tingling sensation in his penis, but while on one level he would like to possess her, on another level he is not ready to touch her. The time has not come; the ripeness is not there. He simply enjoys her scent and her shape and a slight anticipation of further touch.

Leeda looks at the shell but is more aware of the man's eyes on her. She feels the old sensation of being undressed by a man's eyes, but on this occasion she enjoys being so watched. Without admitting it to herself, she feels that nakedness before him would be not embarrassing but delightful.

They walk on to the hotel in full silence but close communion. At the door she considers giving him a quick kiss in gratitude for her rescue. But she rejects the notion: she is already too close to him for that.

単戈

Since a fight is an act of love, judo as a fighting art is also an art of loving. It is easier to see that a fight must be an act of love than to see that an act of love must be a fight—indeed the latter is not quite true, for it is love that includes war. Venus takes Mars into herself finally. But just as there are similarities between men and women, there are parallels between love and war: in both one hurts and is hurt, is in some respects destroyed and reborn as a new creature, and may know both pleasure and pain. The Judoka approaches and conducts himself in love exactly as he does in war.

The events of the walk back to the hotel constitute a complete love scene. It is a complete act of love despite the fact that it is not consummated, that the man hardly touches the woman.

The notion that lovemaking does not begin until the penis enters the vagina, that what occurs before is "preliminary" or "foreplay" having value only in heightening the sensation of coitus, is absurd. Carried one step further, only the orgasm is of consequence, and everything else is simply "put up with" for its sake. Carried still a bit further—as I'm afraid it often is—even the orgasm drops out: all that matters is having made the girl or having satisfied the wife.(The word *satisfied* in this context is an interesting and terrifying one. To think that the very goal of sex and human intercourse should be reduced to the level of what is "satisfactory"!)

Reflected in the Judoka's conduct is a state of mind precisely opposite to that which produces notions of relative importance. If during his walk he had seen into the future and learned that his courtship was going nowhere, would never reach consummation, he would have changed nothing in his behavior. Nor would he have regarded the courtship as a waste of time. In fact, he did regard the evening walk as an entity in and of itself and having as purpose only its own existence. The Judoka understands what Wallace Stevens means in saying that death is the mother of beauty—that those things that are ephemeral take on added luster. He knows that every day and every evening walk are ephemeral, that they pass on never to be repeated; thus he is accustomed to regard every day and every event as being its own fulfillment. William Blake has written:

> He who binds to himself a joy
> Does the winged life destroy,
> But he who kisses the joy as it flies
> Lives in eternity's sunrise.

The third line pretty well describes the Judoka's conduct.

The consummation of fighting is killing; the consummation of courtship is impregnating. The Judoka has this day neither killed anyone nor impregnated anyone. Yet he has both fought and loved, known both pain and pleasure in the one and almost pure pleasure in the other. If neither event has any further ramification, he is satisfied with the day. He has lived.

Our national overconcern about orgasm and sexual accomplishment is an instance of our general cultural confusion about means and ends. We tend to regard the end or accomplishment as all important, the means or processes of accomplishment as significant only insofar as they work—*to work* meaning just to arrive at a satisfactory end. We tend to forget that life is made up of means, not ends, and that to have one's attention always caught up in the finish of the current activity is never to have it caught up in one's actual present life at all. Or, more accurately, it is to distort the present life into something less delightful (and less painful—the two cannot be separated) than it would otherwise be. All of this is not to suggest that ends are not important; they are exactly as important as means. But not more important.

One advantage of shifting some attention from ends to means is that ends are likely to be of more value when attention is paid to means than when attention is concentrated on the ends themselves. This point is easy enough to understand, but it is most clearly apparent in arts like dance or judo in which means and ends come together. My contention is that love is one of those arts and that courtship has the same relation to orgasm that the first bars of a symphony have to the final crescendo.

That the Judoka does not taste the young woman's lips or touch her skin more than lightly is less important than we customarily consider it. After all, more of his senses are involved than are not involved in enjoying her. He neither tastes her nor touches her in more than what might be a casual manner, but he does catch her scent and hear her and look at her. Too, there is in operation that other sense by which both he and she recognize the rapport, the atmosphere, between them. By a four-to-two margin (not counting the touching of hands) the Judoka's lovemaking is a sensuous affair.

The atmosphere, the vibrations, and that other sense are *real*, by the way. Nineteenth-century science, and twentieth-century popular realism following it, tried to reduce reality to the mechanical and things like sixth sense to the realm of superstition. But now we find that they reduced too much. Our scientific theory now tells us that there is more void than anything else between the electrons and that electrons are fictions anyway—we may regard them as waves or particles, whichever is more convenient. Apparently we read in much of what we call reality, participate in it, as our eyes participate in the creation of a rainbow. Reality, then, may be even simpler than we thought it was; it may be simply the process. But the process itself may be more complex than we thought it was, and it is certainly deeper. It may be that whatever is experienced is for that reason real. For the present, that seems the best usage of the word.

The Judoka's basic attitude toward the woman is precisely the same as it is toward the men he fights. When she wants to talk, he is pleased to have her talk; when she is quiet, he enjoys the quietness. When she shows special qualities worthy of delight—her intelligence and artistic sensitivity and good judgment and poise—he delights in them. When she stops to look at a seashell, he too looks at the seashell. He not only lets her do what she wishes, neither blocking nor pushing, but he also turns what she does to his own— and her own, their mutual—advantage. Thus he yields to her just as he does to the redhead and the tall man.

Although the Judoka possesses considerable detachment, he still desires the young woman. In fact, his desire is greater than the average man's in proportion to his greater detachment. The reason that he does not grasp or even want to grasp after her is that his desire is linked on both ends to just what he is already getting. He desires and fulfills his desire at once, as one motion.

None of this is absolute, of course. (If any of it were, the Judoka would be no longer human and Leeda would have no interest in him. What I'm showing is the *direction* in which the Judoka differs from ordinary men.) There are times when the Judoka is hungry and has nothing to eat, and there are times when he would like the touch of a woman but has no woman. But even on these occasions, his turn of mind is to accept the deprivation and in a crazy sort of way to enjoy the pain. In the case of food, he also hunts.

He never hunts for a woman, either in the manner of a man seeking a wife or in that of a boy seeking weekend diversion. For the quest of the latter for ego satisfaction and pressure on the penis, the Judoka has near contempt. If he cannot love a woman—if she is not a *person* whom he can love and in whom he can lose himself—he does not wish to "have" her. But he has no wish either to hold a woman and bind her to him, to get her to promise to love him forever as if she could predict and control whether and what she is going to love. (The Judoka would not know whether or not he could love her forever. He does not know whom or what he may love on any tomorrow. He has no assurance that he can love any enemy who comes along. And he may suffer badly some day for that incapacity.)

Like all men, the Judoka many times has a profound need for the presence of and rapport with another human being; like most men, he finds that need satisfied more completely by women than by other men. When he finds himself in this condition he is, if not actively looking, at least alert for feminine companionship. What he wants is just what he has in this evening walk along the beach: a woman he can respect and like and love; union with her in whatever fashion and to whatever degree the situation offers more or less of itself.

The Judoka feels a tingling in his penis after, not before, he feels a rapport with the young woman in silence, in conversation, and in study of the shells. It is this rapport, this atmosphere, that he is waiting to let ripen, although it is already a more mature and ecstatic thing than many couples know when they are already in bed. He knows that when that rapport comes to full expression, if it ever does, his body and mind and spirit will be ready and yearning, and so will hers, and their coming together will happen almost of itself. The consummation will be devout in the full meaning of that term—sacramental, holy, a thing of great and natural beauty and truth. This is the only kind of sex in which the Judoka is interested.

Leeda's theory of imaginative play relates to both the ripening process of love and the nature of the reality of the consummation. The slowness of the ripening process, the gradual approach of two people to each other, permits the imagination of each to play on the still-unexplored aspects of the other—physical aspects, but also mental and emotional aspects.

In saying this, I do not mean anything so crude and undesirable as that the man will fancy the woman's breasts as more shapely than they really are or her personality more interesting than it really is. What I mean is quite the antithesis of that. The play of imagination on the person permits one to see more fully, more clearly, and more poetically what is really there, and indeed to heighten—without in the least intending or desiring to modify—the very reality itself.

Blake made a similar point when he said that he saw the sun, not as the scientists do, as a kind of bright coin in the sky, but as a host of flaming angels. I once thought this expression a mere poetic exaggeration, but now I am convinced that it is a simple statement of fact: the sun, as experienced by Blake, *was* a host of flaming angels. And for me to prefer the coin-sun, the sun of Newton's Sleep, to Blake's is for me to adopt a least-common-denominator concept of the world, as if the color and perspective of the world were "really" what the average man sees rather than what the great painter sees. Most of us grant theoretically the possibility of man's participation in the structure of reality; but most of us still act as if reality were just the lowest common denominator of the sciences, and in our "realistic" moods think of it that way. We need not do so.

A simple instance of imagination affecting reality in a valuable way occurs when a man falls in love with a woman and begins to see her in his own mind's eye as more attractive and desirable and indeed beautiful—in a very "real" sense—than other women whose features, he realizes, would be more likely to attract the attention of a glamour photographer.

Another way of putting all this is to say that the man who lets his imagination play on the woman is likely to see her as a full person, with her potential actualized, rather than as a reduced person. He deals with her as whole person instead of as sex object or companion or playmate or whatever. And it is just this relating to her as whole person—which is to say as *person*—that affects the nature of the consummation. As everyone who has had both kinds of experience knows, sexual congress between *persons* is a far, far different thing, even physically, from that between sex objects.

Since this book presumes to be a treatise on judo, it is perhaps in order to point out that what is true in love regarding this matter is also true in strife, although the circumstances of a fight usually rule out the possibility of gradual approach. In the case of the fight, it is easier to see the effects of imagination in negative terms than in positive ones. When one knows that a fight is coming up, one's fear is likely to grow in anticipation until the adversary has grown disproportionately awesome and terrifying. But what if one should learn to love his enemy, so that the love finally dominates the fear?

Leeda's interest in a combination of dance and poetry contrasts with her mother's satisfaction with the poem alone.

To merely hear or merely see a poem—and I suspect that is the way they have usually been experienced—is to experience it, to live the portion of one's life that is devoted to the poem, with only a small part of the person. Leeda wants to experience the poem more fully, with her whole person; no doubt she wants to experience all else that comes her way similarly. What she wants, then, is a less sedentary or partial life than her parents had. No doubt one reason, among several, for the Judoka's adoption of his life style is that it permits him a less sedentary, and therefore more nearly full, existence than he could obtain living more conventionally.

# HUNTING

On his way back to camp the Judoka's mind is filled with images and thoughts, mostly of Leeda—her way of choosing a hotel, her way of regarding her art, her voice, her long jet-black hair and her way of brushing it aside, her shape, whether or not she will show up for the judo lessons. He thinks too of the fight, the redhead and the tall man and the two fellows who no doubt are now embarrassed because they did not fight. He lets the random thoughts run. Slowly they bubble off and his mind grows still. The night is quiet.

Arriving at his camp, he thinks about eating but rejects the notion: he really isn't hungry enough to hunt. He strips off all his clothes, folds them neatly, and lays them across a couple of heavy lower branches of one of the bushes. Naked, he walks outside the ring of bushes to a spot about forty feet down the beach. The air feels good against his bare skin.

He scoops out a few handfuls of sand and squats over the depression, his knees against his chest. Gradually and pleasurably, he lets his feces return to the earth. Although he is staring out to sea, he is paying very little attention to the sea; his attention is centered on the relief and new lightness in his bowels. He understands why the bowels were long considered the seat of compassion. Finished, he wets his hand from a bottle filled with seawater and cleans himself, although the consistency of his stool is such that he needs very little cleaning. He pitches sand into the hole, rinses his hands, and returns to the enclosure.

He puts the bottle of seawater near some freshwater containers in an apple crate lying on its side to serve as a kind of cabinet. This crate occupies an inverted-V-shaped opening formed by two of the thicker bushes. On its top sits a kerosene lamp, which the Judoka now lights. He kneels before the crate, both knees to the ground, haunches on heels, big toes crossed. From the crate he pulls out a library copy of *Moby Dick*, lays it on top of the crate, and reads.

For a considerable period of time he reads, pausing occasionally to stare out into the dark toward the water. Once he wonders if his dancer could interpret Queequeg poised with a harpoon. Then he stops to stretch; his first stretch not quite satisfying him, he lays out a bedroll, kneels on it for a moment, and then goes up into a headstand. He remains in that posture for a short while, noticing, although not for the first time, that even the stars look different from an uncommon point of view. He wonders if Ahab's point of view affects him physically, if it could be danced. He rolls out gently, returns to the crate, and resumes reading.

Finally he quits reading, douses the lamp, and stretches out on his back on the bedroll. Immediately everything in his mind is wiped away and replaced by the glittering beauty of the stars. He is far enough from town and near enough to the ocean that neither city lights nor dust obscures their brightness. Although he sees these stars in the same way virtually every night, he does not get used to them; they still dazzle him. Easily and rather quickly, he falls asleep.

He lies rather still, on his back for the most part, but once in a while on his stomach. His sleep is light but not restless, except for a short period during an unpleasant dream. The dream awakens him momentarily, but then he realizes what has happened and settles back to sleep and lets the dream continue if it will.

As the dawn breaks to the southeast over the water, he begins to awaken. He actually awakens with the morning; as the light increases and the birds begin to stir, he begins to stir also. The process is a slow and smooth one. He does not wake up deliberately; he just lets the morning rouse him. In his earlier life he hated conversation and radio music early in the morning; now he feels the same way about thinking. Early in the morning he wants simply to be. He gives no thought at all to what he is going to do when he gets up. He just lies on his back listening to the occasional call of a seabird and watching the sky grow gray and then red and then yellow and then blue.

狩

Empedocles thought that Love and Strife were basic substances and that they, with fire and air and earth and water, constitute that which is everlasting—that which is, being itself. Now, with our scientific and philosophic and poetic theories that energy is what is and that objects are merely patterns in that energy gross enough to be perceivable to man through his five senses, we can almost drop out the traditional four elements and otherwise go along with Empedocles. In any event, there seems to be a genuine sense in which love and strife constitute being.

In our culture being is almost always underplayed in favor of becoming. We could paraphrase Pope and say, "Man never is but always to become." This situation is almost surprising in view of our usual greater interest in ends than in means. (It's not really surprising: we're never greatly interested in an end we have already attained.) Perhaps this is our way of compensating: In order to make up for our customary neglect of means, we perform the equal and opposite absurdity in this instance of making everything means and having no end in view!

To want to be always becoming, and never to be satisfied with simply being, is as nonsensical as wanting to freeze life and hold it and prevent it from becoming anything other than what it is—which is another thing we do. The only important point here is the effect our way of regarding being and becoming has on our attitudes and modes of conduct, for it seems unlikely that what we think (about this matter) is going to affect the fundamental situation: being is always becoming, in that everything is in constant flux, and becoming is simply one form of being.

But our ways of regarding these matters do affect our attitudes and our behavior. One of the chief differences between the Judoka and most other people is that he is far more interested in being than in becoming. Ironically, sleep, which is one corner of pure being, has the function of renewing the person and is therefore an almost pure becoming, so that the Judoka, who knows how to be and thus sleeps well, does a better job of becoming (while sleeping) than the man who "tries to" sleep in order to "work well" the next day.

What is true of sleep in this respect is also true of the waking state. The child does not grow by trying to grow but simply by being a child. Similarly, it is not the man bent on constant self-improvement who develops into a fully mature human being, but the man who is content to be what he is.

I intend to discuss this matter, but before I do so, I must remind the reader that no statement is ever wholly true—including the one I just made. There is some virtue in learning and even in what we ordinarily call "self-improvement," but that virtue is not quite what we think it is when we regard these activities in a superficial manner. Everything depends upon the *attitude* in which we engage in them.

In an essay called "Zen and the Problem of Control," Alan Watts shows how our efforts at self-control are hampered by what he calls a kind of "double-bind." When a person tries to break a "bad" habit like smoking or overeating, it sometimes happens that his "higher nature"—his conscious mind—fails to exert adequate control over his "lower nature"—his body. Since the body is as much the self as the mind (higher and lower not meaning much in practice) this conflict amounts to a person's attempt to go two ways at once. Consequently, he goes nowhere at all. This is the double-bind: each part of the person is working against the other. A solution to this quandary is not easy either to understand or to accomplish, Watts admits, but it lies in a kind of judo, (Watts uses that word; I am not interpreting.) This judo takes the form of a turning in the direction of the fall as a bicyclist or a skidding motorist does. The idea is to release the paralysis of the will: "Man cannot control himself unless he accepts himself. . . . Before he can change his course of action he must first be sincere, going with and not against his nature, even when the immediate trend of his nature is toward evil, toward a fall."

A later and simpler statement of the principle appears in Arnold Veisser's essay, "The Paradoxical Theory of Change," published in a volume called *Gestalt Therapy Now.* Veisser's thesis is *that change occurs when one becomes what he is, not when he tries to become what he is not.*

These men seem to be suggesting that a person give up strict diets and abstention from smoking, in short that he quit trying to improve; that instead he content himself with doing what he has to do, or in other words, with being what he is. To put the matter in still other words, they suggest that a person yield to his own strongest desires—to eat, say, or to smoke. I think it consistent with their position to suggest that the person really let himself enjoy the smoking or the eating, enjoy them more than he ever has. Once he does this, and settles into being, change is not only possible but inevitable.

This technique is far removed from any magic trick enabling a person to outsmart his "lower" nature and fool himself into not wanting cigarettes or food. Indeed, to attempt such a trick would insure failure.

It should also be noted that the judo here, if it works at all, will work like judo as a fighting art. When Kano's seven-unit man yields to the ten-unit man, the two people do not go in the direction toward which the seven-unit man was originally pushing. They go nearly, but not quite, in the opposite direction, but with the seven-unit man on top. So with the person who yields to his lower nature: he does not necessarily get where he originally wanted to go, but he goes in what is effectively an altogether new direction. Presumably, the new direction is one in which he is wise to go.

Let's suppose that a man who smokes cigarettes to excess tries to quit and fails. He decides to try this judo approach. He notes that "he" did not really want to quit: his conscious mind and his mouth perhaps (tired of the bad taste) wanted to quit, but some stronger part or parts of him did not share the desire. Clearly the cigarettes have value for that part or those parts; thus, for "him." At this point he may be able to identify the need being served and see how to satisfy it without smoking, or he may even see that the need itself is illusory, an outgrowth of a superstitious belief that he cannot quit. However, the chances are that his problem is not to be this simply solved, so he goes on to the next step. He accepts the conclusion that the cigarettes have value for him, and—here's the nearly impossible part—he sincerely and utterly gives up the effort and the desire to quit smoking. He lets himself really enjoy the cigarettes, and he is alert to what he is enjoying. Being alert, he may soon learn that his senses really appreciate but very few of the cigarettes, for even perverted senses do not respond with genuine delight to excess. (Hence the bad taste in his mouth, of which he has long been aware.) He may learn too that the part of his person that really demands the excessive intake is not so much a mysterious lower self as a kind of middle being that exists somewhere between the threatening outside world and an even more threatening and untrustworthy "self" that seems to reside deep within his own person. But this middle being is strong only when the man is engaged in abstract thought—usually of past or future—and the man cannot now do much of this kind of thinking, at least not while he is smoking, for appreciation of the tobacco demands that he focus on present taste and aroma. Having escaped his anxiety about a future absence of tobacco, he may at times get playful and just for fun refuse to light up and, still playfully, take note of his reactions, the dryness in the throat or whatever. He may come to appreciate the observation experience just as he does the tobacco experience. Focusing his attention on his own person rather than on the cigarettes he wants, he may notice that his suffering is less severe than he once thought it and that this heightened awareness in austerity is itself a game worth playing occasionally. Smoking again and paying attention to his "selves" and to the outside world (from which the smoke is coming), he may, since he is enjoying and not wishing to interfere, come to have sympathy not only for the selves but for that threatening outside world that upon close inspection turns out to be just another of his selves. Paying close and sympathetic attention to all of these entities, he may come to observe, and by feeling-with to understand, the curious manner in which they work with and against one another, and he may even have to laugh. At this point he may, by getting the feel of being off balance, learn what it is like to be centered in both body and mind—and if he does, he likes the feeling and keeps returning to it. Now he grows much more acutely aware of what he is doing, and even through his continuing laughter he may realize that some elements of his selves are wanting to live while others are wanting to die and that those wanting to live can do so only if those wanting to die can die—and that those wanting to die can do so only in great pain. He may now have to cry out for help, asking for someone to help him kill or, if that's not possible, to love him. If there is no one available, he may have to seek aid from the very selves in which he consists, especially that external self containing trees and grasses against which he can rub. If he survives, he may laugh again, this time in delight. He may come to understand that falling is as rich an experience as rising, that whatever is flawed is for that reason perfect, and that pain is fully as glorious as pleasure. So it may be that now he has little to fear and so no need to protect his middle self from threats within and without and so no need to consume nervously more cigarettes than the few he can fully appreciate.

All of this is mere speculation, a hypothetical case of a particular man with a particular weakness—not, however, an uncommon kind of weakness—and it is at best an outline of a conceivable kind of experience. The only seriously improbable part of the speculation is that the man is successful in that initial, all-important, terribly frightful letting go.

But if we suppose the man successful this far, we can easily suppose him going on, applying more broadly the principles he has learned, until he is living like the Judoka, doing exactly what he wants to do all of the time, never suffering the double-bind, making no effort at becoming what he is not, being what he is, sleeping when he feels like sleeping, waking up when he feels like waking up, standing on his head when that activity seems inviting—and smoking a cigarette appreciatively when he is in the mood. His smoking is now an experience that raises, rather than lowers, his level of consciousness, and is actually of positive value to him.

Nevertheless, it should be noted that he has failed in his original intention. Failed beautifully.

Perhaps the principle to be recognized here is that a person may be wise to avoid desire to change himself and yet not fear to let himself change—that he may be wise rather to appreciate what is, including his own being, letting his intellect and will play their parts in determining his destiny but remembering that they too are flawed and do not deserve to be in absolute control.

The Judoka has been living by this Way of Appreciation long enough to do it easily. We see him doing it in his daydreaming and random thinking on his walk back from the hotel. He knows the value of no-mind, of being in the here-and-now, but he does not make a fetish or an obsession of maintaining that state. When it feels good to think or day-dream, he thinks or daydreams, provided there is no pressing circumstance to prevent his doing so.

There is a slight difference in the situation when he gets home. He would like to eat, but having no refrigerator, he would have to go out and hunt for food, and he does not want to go hunting. Thus, he is less likely than most of us to confuse appetite—the desire for food induced by habit or by the nervous wish to nibble during a television program—with true hunger. Consequently, he has no weight problem.

He does defecate when he gets home. Naked, he has none of the humiliating and sordid feeling of having trousers and drawers down around his ankles and knees. He has his knees up against his chest so that he can void properly. To clean himself, he uses water, which feels better than paper, leaves no litter, and is less likely to cause hemorrhoids. He does not need much cleaning: his diet and life style are such that his stool has the consistency of that of a healthy animal.

The Judoka sees nothing dirty or degrading about defecation. He recognizes it not only as a biological necessity but also as a sensuous experience similar in several respects to orgasm. He gives it his full attention, delights in it; he is little more likely to read during defecation than he is to read during orgasm. In addition, he regards his feces as the product of his person, the only product (other than his urine and perhaps a little of his semen and his spittle or his vomit and bits of fingernails, toenails, and hair) that he returns to the earth while he lives in exchange for the material sustenance he draws from it. He regards his stool as a kind of offering.

Life is process. It may be that process is even the correct name of the gods. One phase of process is taking in and putting out. Neither of these can exist without the other, and neither has more dignity or deserves more respect than the other. In this scene we see the Judoka taking in by reading and putting out by defecating. That one of these is "mental" and the other "physical" makes no difference. Perhaps on another occasion he will eat and talk.

The Judoka does not go to sleep with the night, and in this respect he is perhaps a little unnatural, as most civilized men are. But we are faced with another paradox here. As René Dubos shows in his *Mirage of Health*, man can never be quite "harmonious with nature" in the same way that the lower animals are; it is part of the "nature" of man to think and experiment and vary from the instinctive practices of other creatures. This does not mean that man should give up his attempts to swim with the current, but only that he should realize that imperfection is built into his very being. One of the main themes of Joseph Conrad is that the very characteristics that make man fully human tend to destroy him. But this too can be accepted. It is neither good nor bad. It is just the way the world is.

The Judoka sleeps lightly because he does not need a great deal of profound sleep. His variety of activities, both mental and physical, over the course of the day provides contraction and relaxation for most of his muscles and places undue stress on few of them.

While the Judoka does not go to sleep with the night, he does wake up with the morning. Sleeping outdoors and far enough from city lights to experience the dazzling beauty of the stars, he undergoes, both in going to sleep and in awakening with the dawn, what Abraham Maslow calls *peak experience*. Maslow has written that peak experiences may have a significant effect on mental and consequent physical health. Colin Wilson has speculated that they have philosophic significance as well-that they are necessary to a genuine understanding of the world.

The Judoka's awakening process is merely another instance of his abandoning himself to whatever activity presently engages him. He does not sacrifice the quiet ecstasy of a gentle awakening to anticipation of the business of the day. After all, what greater can he attain by the business of the day than what he is already experiencing?

狩

The Judoka stretches deeply preparatory to getting up, his arms straight up in the air. At the instant that his vision is blocked by his upraised arm, the woman in the yellow bathing suit steps into the enclosure. She sees the naked man against a backdrop of white sand and bright-green, dewy shrubbery. She is fascinated and not the least bit embarrassed. And when, a minute later, he sees her, she feels no need to act embarrassed. She smiles, a bit mischievously. Nor does he jump to cover up. He just grins.

"Hi" he says. "Forgive my informality. I didn't expect a guest.

"Forgive my not knocking," she replies. "I didn't find a door."

"Come in and sit down, he says, indicating the bedroll as he rises and steps into a bathing suit. "How about a cup of coffee?"

She nods assent and sits down.

He extracts from the crate a can with the label removed. He pours water into the can, lights the kerosene lamp, and then places the can above the fire by means of a rig constructed out of a coathanger. Next he takes from the crate a small dripolator, a shell about the size and shape of a small dish, and a smooth rock. In addition, he pulls out a sack of coffee beans. Putting the beans in the shell, he then uses the rock as a pestle and grinds them. Leeda watches this procedure in amazement. The Judoka finishes his grinding about the time the water boils, and soon he has the drip process going. Then he takes from the crate a pair of Naritake china cups.

"China cups?" she says.

"I'm a sensuous man," he replies. "I once read a newspaper columnist who said that he had never drunk good coffee out of a paper or plastic cup. My experience is the same."

The coffee tastes better than any Leeda has ever had. Perhaps the fresh sea air has something to do with it, she thinks. She explains that she has come for judo lessons, realizing as she does that she has a rather weak excuse for such an early visit. However, he takes her explanation at face value and asks if she has plenty of time. She says that she has.

"Come on then and we'll get some breakfast," he says. He takes her hand and walks straight out to the ocean. In his other hand is a ring net, the ring made out of three coathangers twisted tightly together, and a net that is simply a sack.

He asks if she can swim, and she says yes. He plunges with her out into the water and swims out a considerable distance. She swims very well indeed, gracefully, as she walks. No doubt she will play judo the same way eventually, the Judoka tells himself.

Finally the Judoka touches down on a sandbar that permits Leeda to keep her head barely above the water. He asks her to hold the sack net, then he plunges down into the water to hunt. He emerges with nothing. The couple moves to the next sandbar and then to another and then to another. The Judoka does not hurry; he acts as if his only purpose were sightseeing in the fantasy world beneath the surface. Then, as they are swimming on the surface, he suddenly yells—and for an amused instant pretends that he is in the crow's nest of the *Pequod*—and dives down to the bottom into a school of blue crabs. Leeda follows him down. He collects crabs with the ring net and makes fairly intricate transfers to the sack. After coming up for air six or eight times, the hunters have an appreciable number of crabs.

On the way in to the shore, the Judoka, unhampered apparently by the sack of blue crabs, keeps making short underwater excursions to either side of the course. On the last of these he comes up with a large handful of reddish-purple seaweed. As they emerge from the water, the young woman decides that whatever her food tastes like, she will never have a breakfast more appealing to the eye than the blue crabs and red-purple laver.

The Judoka leaves the crabs with Leeda at the camp and takes the seaweed and a bucket to a nearby freshwater well. He returns with washed seaweed, a bucket of water for boiling, and a supply of dewberries.

Having had a long walk and a hard swim before the strange breakfast, Leeda is not sure whether the boiled crab, laver, dewberries, and newly ground coffee make such an excellent meal because they are much fresher than anything she ordinarily eats or just because she is so very hungry.

"This is a magnificent meal," she says, "but you must use a great deal of time getting food."

The Judoka smiles. "Not a lot more time than it would take sitting around an office long enough to get money to buy frozen food at a supermarket," he says. "Besides, I find seahunting an activity of value for its own sake."

There is little conversation during the meal. The Judoka's manner does not encourage it, although he is relaxed and easy and pleasant. He has pulled everything from the crate and laid the box itself across the bedroll in such manner that he and Leeda can eat not quite opposite each other. The Judoka eats in a kneeling

75

posture, the same one he uses for reading. He eats deliberately, although not especially slowly. There is no silverware, and the food must be taken by hand. The Judoka seems to regard this as an advantage. He takes the texture of the crabmeat and the seaweed as he brings it to his mouth. With the dewberries and the coffee, he pauses almost imperceptibly to catch the aroma.

Surreptitiously, the woman glances at him from time to time, trying not to be impolite. His attitude toward the food in his mouth seems to be a curious mixture of the cold, controlled savagery of yesterday's fight and the warm tenderness of the caress a man might give a woman.

狩

Thoreau argues in *Walden* that he can travel across the country on foot faster than his neighbor can by train. It is thirty miles to Fitchburg, he writes, and he can walk that distance in a day. The train fare is approximately a day's wage. "Well, I start now . . . and get there before night . . . You will in the meanwhile have earned your fare, and arrive there sometime tomorrow . . . And so, if the railroad reached round the world, I think that I should keep ahead of you; and as for seeing the country and getting experience of that kind, I should have cut your acquaintance altogether."

Like much of what Thoreau writes, the logic is so sound and the argument so powerful that one wonders why it has taken the world over a hundred years to begin to understand what the man had to say. The Judoka's hunting is simply his way of applying Thoreau's principle to the essential task of getting food.

It is still possible to live by hunting, especially if one is alert to plants as well as animals, as Bradford Angier and Euell Gibbons have shown in various books describing their own experiences. Gibbons once prepared a gourmet dinner made up entirely of wild foods gathered in one morning in Central Park, New York City, at a not especially favorable time of year!

On first thought it may seem that hunting every day for one's food might become as drudging an occupation as pumping gasoline or clerking in a grocery store, but a little reflection suggests that this is not the case. Since a man who is hungry wants to get something to eat, and since the Judoka hunts only when he is hungry, the Judoka as hunter is doing what he most wants to do at the particular moment—and doing it directly, not indirectly as he would be if he were working for money to exchange for food. This argument may seem specious, but it isn't. However, I mention it only as preliminary to a couple of other points. One of these is that hunger increases awareness, thus making the Judoka a better hunter than he would otherwise be, and, more importantly, making him more *alive* than he would otherwise be, for increased awareness is a defining characteristic of being more fully alive. The other point— which is really just a slightly different aspect of the first—is that hunting is an adventurous occupation. An anthropologist has written that the savage who woke up hungry and never knew whether or not he was going to get to eat was never bored; he adds that our civilized food-getting activities—usually for next month—do not have that immediacy and thus lack the thrill of the savage's hunt. O. Henry has written that there is no comparison between the pleasure felt by a millionaire who has just made another million and the intense joy of a destitute man who has just found a quarter. The idea is the same.

Men seem to desire both security and adventure. Under primitive conditions, security is quite unattainable and adventure is plentiful. Under our highly civilized conditions, long range security is still unattainable, but we manage to gain temporary and substitute partial securities (money for next month's food, insurance, etc.). And under either primitive or civilized conditions we can by our thinking gain certain kinds of security—by identifying with nature or the gods. We seem to require some security, but when we get too much of it (whether true or false) we sacrifice much of the possibility of adventure. And this doesn't work out well; when our lives are without adventure we feel frustration, which sometimes explodes, as when the pastor runs off with the lead soprano. As in judo, where one defends oneself best precisely by not being too defensive, it may be that the only true security is to be found in adventure.

Variety in anything attacks boredom; variety of or within occupation attacks drudgery. Seasonal maturation and scarcity of single species ensure that the hunter, especially one hunting sea foods and wild plants, must engage himself in various ways and with various goals. It may be too that variety is the key to other things besides interest—proper diet, for example—and that the wild food hunter necessarily avoids the ill effects of oversimplification of diet that seems to cause problems for both those people who eat standard foods and those who follow health systems. But perhaps the most important variation provided by the Judoka's somewhat primitive occupation and life style is that between comfort and discomfort. In the Nightgown chapter of *Moby Dick* Ishmael points out that the person who can afford to keep a fire burning in his bedroom misses the highly pleasurable contrast between warm bed and icy bedroom. The principle is that to be too comfortable at all times and in all ways is to miss entirely the highest of pleasures. Applying the principle positively (by necessity), the Judoka's stoicism becomes epicureanism! Yet he avoids—is indeed at the opposite pole from—that kind of luxury Thoreau had in mind when he wrote that "of a life of luxury the fruit is luxury, whether in agriculture, or commerce, or literature, or art."

Willingness to live primitively if necessary is perhaps even more important than actually doing it, for this willingness is essential to independence. Charles Reich argues in The Greening of America that one of the marks of the typical American who matured soon after the end of the Second World War is a fear of dropping out of the established order, a fear that he will become a "non-person" if he does so. A person must either never have this fear or overcome it if he is to be independent. If a man feels that he will not necessarily starve and die and become a non-person if he drops out of the organization—if he even feels that he might be better off to do so—he need not cringe before an employer and sacrifice his integrity and his manhood for security. Unless a person has independence, by definition he is not free. Until he is free, he cannot be whole. Until he is whole, he has no chance of being happy.

Independence of this kind is really not so much independence at all; it is dependence, not on any one thing and certainly not on an established organization, but on everything. (So independence and dependence parallel detachment and attachment.) Another word for it is *faith*.

This confidence in the essential buoyancy of life makes it possible for a person to conduct his activities in the spirit that a recent writer has called *high play*. As I understand this high play, it is activity based on a consciousness that the mountain as well as the feet of the climber carry the climber up the mountain—and so it is activity conducted seriously yet in a mood of playfulness, activity that makes one aware of value yet does not make one compulsive, activity in which one engages but still stands aside and wonders at the game. The person who lives continually in a spirit of high play or as if he were a dramatic character (Churchill with his consciousness of history might be an example) lives as if he were a contestant in a game. He plays to win, but he is not oppressed by an overestimation of the ultimate consequence of his victory or defeat. (In other words, he lives as the Judoka or the Zen swordsman fights.) The attitude of low play is that of Ahab, in which there can be no playfulness because the stakes are too great.

The play, the pretending, of the child is not quite the same thing as high play, yet it is a parallel, an elementary version of it. Children's play does for the child something like what interpretive dance does for Leeda: it enables the person to live a mythic moment, to impart high drama to something that might otherwise be mundane, to restore to the world some of the glory lost in man's usual reductionist attitude. There can be considerable value in this kind of pretending for adults too, but most adults cannot engage in it (except perhaps in amateur theater, which may explain the popularity of that pastime) because doing so seems silly. The Judoka, of course, does not permit any such consideration to influence him. Without analyzing why he wants to do it, he lets himself pretend for an instant that he is a *Pequod* lookout sighting whale, and in so doing lets himself feel the thrill of a poetic moment.(Melville does much the same thing for his reader by describing whaling in terms of military glories.) In making that small gesture the Judoka takes a giant step in the direction of the spirit of high play.

The Judoka tends to be as playful in dealing with deadly serious matters as he is in dealing with rather casual ones. This playfulness is easy to misunderstand, especially for those of us who have been urged since birth to "work hard" and "try harder," but it is essential to understand for the person who would play judo well or be successful in almost any line of endeavor. The playfulness I have in mind—the spirit of high play—is a little like that of the mathematician playing with numbers or the poet toying with puns; yet even these examples may distort my meaning. Perhaps I will do best to point to my own work—to this book you are presently reading. There are passages in this book that I am having to work my way through; there are others that I do easily, that are simply fun for me to do. If you are a perceptive reader, if you have a feel for style and flow, you can distinguish the extreme examples of each. The far better ones are those that it is fun for me to do.

In hunting, the Judoka looks for what is ripe—for what *wants* to be eaten. (One destroys in eating as one destroys in loving; but one who is loved takes pleasure in being destroyed to create the beast with two backs. Would it be possible to imagine the ripe fruit as enjoying a sort of consummation in the act of being destroyed as it is becoming part of a human being, as it is being made human? The notion seems like poetic pleasantry, yet it is not a hard one to believe, and I see more good than harm in believing it.)

The Judoka is guided in his hunting, as in his eating, by what smells and tastes good. This is his chief way of determining what plants and fish are edible. Books on the subject of hunting wild foods usually advise eating only plants one knows by name and characteristics, and for the average person, with his lack of awareness and his perverted tastes, this is no doubt good counsel; but I see no reason for it to be necessary for a man like the Judoka. There seems little likelihood that his taste buds will mislead him. (Even those of the average man warn him of more sweets, which still "taste good," when he has had too many sweets.) At

Summerhill, A. S. Neill never forced any child to eat anything. Many children, after a period of eating all sweets, would go to eating all green beans for a while, until they had restored a balance in their diet. I have a notion that the taste buds, if left unperverted, will guide the mind in its selection of foods according to the body's needs. The Judoka's emphasis on taste insures that he chews correctly, for food really tastes only when adequately chewed, and probably insures that his food is "good for him"—for it is likely that the only kind of food that is healthful is that which is enjoyed.

As important as eating is in its own right, it has great significance beyond itself.

Everything that a person does is a product of the whole person. The person who tends to be contemplative and unhurried in his work tends to be the same way in his manner of talking and walking and eating and everything else he does. This is the person's *style*. (There are variations, of course, in the ways that people do things—a person is more practiced and thus more comfortable in one activity than in another, or he likes one and dislikes another, and so on. But the essential quality or characteristic is the same, generally speaking.)

And just as everything that a person does is a product of his whole being, everything that he does has ramifications for his whole being. If a man customarily gulps down his food, but one day stops and begins deliberately to chew his food thoroughly and savor its taste and enjoy it, the new experience will affect his whole character and personality.

Frederick Perls has paid special attention to the matter of eating in formulating his Gestalt Therapy. In an early work, *Ego, Hunger, and Aggression*, he notes that the kind of person who wants all his food soft—i.e., a person who desires *confluence*—is one who is emotionally still in the breast-feeding stage. He is likely to be a person who sucks contentedly at the breast of mother state or mother corporation for thirty years even if he does not get any real satisfaction from his work. In *Gestalt Therapy*, by Perls with Ralph Hefferline and Paul Goodman, the authors devote considerable attention to the matter of *introjection*. A person who introjects tries to swallow things whole; that is, he takes things into himself—food or reading matter or personal experiences—without really assimilating them. Thus, he does not make them really part of himself, but instead carries around a lot of foreign matter. He lacks internal harmony and is a mockery of a whole person.

The Gestalt Therapists think it worthwhile for a person to observe his own eating habits with these relations in mind. They do *not* recommend that he try suddenly and forcibly to change his habits; only that he be aware of them. The awareness itself is therapeutic, they say.

No doubt Aldous Huxley has in mind the importance of awareness, not only of one's own habits but also of the food itself (awareness being an essential component of love) when he has his Utopians in *Island* "chew grace." They chew the first mouthful until there is nothing left, paying attention to the flavor, consistency, and temperature, pressure on the teeth, feel of the muscles in the jaws. They do not give thanks to God or anyone else while they are doing it, for that would distract attention, and attention is the whole point.

In other words, Huxley sees eating as a sacramental function; sacramental in that it unifies a person with all that is around him, and by extension with the divine, as he takes that which is without him into himself. I myself think it very possible that this is what Jesus had in mind in identifying bread and wine with his own body and blood.

There is a very real and quite natural sense in which everything we eat is the body and blood of Jesus, and is your body and blood and mine too. The sun and the air are as essential to my being as are my heart and lungs. I can no more go off and leave sun and air and water (unless I take some of them with me, as a spacecraft takes oxygen and water) than I can my heart and lungs. The sun and the air and the water, then, are parts of my being. My skin is an arbitrary and conventional boundary. As ecologists are now showing us, what is true of sun and air and water is true— although less directly—of all that exists, the mosquitoes and the snakes and the horses and the lettuce. Thus, everything is already my body and yours and Jesus's. Everything I eat is a communion with you and with Jesus. Ask not for whom the bell tolls.

The taking within what is without occurs in breathing and perception as well as in eating. But eating is more solidly tangible, and serves to symbolize the process as well as to participate in it. If everything that exists is akin to the gods, whatever the gods may be, communion with it is communion with the divine.

狩

Finishing coffee, the Judoka is talkative, and Leeda, pleased, is quick to encourage him. "After that breakfast," she says, "it seems silly to ask this, but I'm going to ask it anyway. Why do you live like this?"

"Had you slept out here last night and seen the stars, you certainly would not have had to ask . . . Yet that's not the whole reason. A couple of years ago, I grew interested in that story about Jesus and the rich young ruler. I had already noticed that most of the things I owned—car that had to be taken to the garage, house with yard to be mowed, suits to be taken to the cleaners—required as much service as they gave me. I began to wonder if Jesus was asking that young ruler for a sacrifice, or if he was just telling him in the simplest way he knew of how one gets into the kingdom of heaven. After considering the matter for a time, I began to wonder if it would be literally possible for a man to consider the lilies of the field or to live like a bird of the air, neither toiling nor spinning but picking up food as it comes to hand."

"Are you—a churchman?" Leeda moves uncomfortably.

"No, not even Christian as the word is usually understood. But I sometimes wonder—did you ever read Chesterton's remark that Christianity hasn't failed, it just hasn't been tried?" The Judoka chuckles softly. "That man is beautiful, the way he takes what you think and pulls you off balance with it. A judo of words . . . But never mind that. Anyway, I just figured that I had an idea what Jesus was trying to tell that man. I decided to give it a try. Then I had another idea. I began reading in ecological articles and decided that most of the business that men do just fouls the environment and doesn't necessarily contribute to human happiness. If people lived like the birds, they wouldn't do as much damage, and if Jesus was right—Anyway, I decided the experiment would be worthwhile."

"And did you find the kingdom of heaven?"

The Judoka laughs. "No, but every now and then I think I'm getting too damned close for comfort." His face grows serious. "Selling out, or rather giving out—hmmn, that could mean something different, couldn't it?—is not the whole answer, I'm sure, but I do think it takes a person part of the way. I've been more comfortable, in a strange but literal sense, sleeping and sitting outdoors and eating dewberries and blue crabs, than I was when I lived conventionally. But that's not the main point. More important is that I don't have errands to run or schedules to meet or people to impress. I can live in the present, the world of the senses, more than I could before; or, if I want to live in the past, I can operate in almost pure memory, not in recall of needed materials; or, in the future, in something like idle speculation rather than plans—or plans if I feel like making them, but not essential plans. Anyway, I find that I can do pretty well what I want to do when I want to do it."

"The life doesn't get boring?" she asks, frowning a bit.

"At first, I kept expecting that to happen, but so far it hasn't. Maybe it's because of the necessary hunting. I have to look at the world around me more closely than I used to, and it, like anything looked at very closely, remains interesting."

Leeda looks thoughtful. "Tell me, do you find that trees, viewed closely—and if one deliberately shuts out of his mind the scientific attitude—are sometimes more than just trees?"

"Indeed I do," the man says. "I find that to some degree I can control whether the tree is 'just' itself or is somehow an expression of all that is. The same is true of books, by the way. Maybe that's why I read a lot—"

"Yes!" Leeda says, sitting bolt upright in delight and becoming for a moment a young girl. "I discovered that a few years ago. The city in which I grew up is primarily industrial, and I thought it was boring, because when I'd look down a street at a row of houses I thought I knew what was going on behind all the doors—the same thing: an old man in his undershirt drinking beer and reading a newspaper while his stringy-haired wife mopped the floor. Once I visited a cousin in a university town, and there I looked at a row of doors and imagined that all sorts of interesting things were going on behind them—somebody inventing a machine, somebody else writing a novel, a coed being seduced, and so on. Well, when I took up the study of English, I discovered that in my hometown I had been what is called in literary terms a *Realist* with a capital R. In the university town I had been a *Romantic*, again with a capital R. But by that time I had learned that I was wrong about both cities: more was going on in one place and less in the other than I had imagined. So I concluded that Realism and Romanticism were both wrong. Or, looking at it the other way, were both right. If that's true, it's better to be a Romanticist, because it's more fun. So ever since I've been a Romanticist by choice, and now I'm beginning to decide that Romanticism is nearer the truth than Realism anyway. I think Realism became important because of its name."

The Judoka cannot reply to all this without thinking it over, but the girl does not give him time. "The only thing that bothers me about this life style of yours, doing whatever you want, is that it is undisciplined." Her voice has a lilt; she is teasing, although she is serious.

The Judoka shakes his head. "You try doing just exactly what you really want to do just exactly when you want to do it for a little while. You will find it is, as Gary Snyder puts it, the hardest discipline of all. All your habits of body and mind interfere."

This time Leeda does not reply, and the Judoka continues: "The value of it, I think, lies in something like this: Once you remove the sort of crust of habitual forcing, your body or your mind—your person—will tell you when you need to eat or sleep or exercise or make love. Consequently, if you are free to do what you want, and you form the habit of doing it, you get along all right. It amounts to a kind of faith in life, a letting your weight down, so to speak. It happens in judo; what a person has to learn to do—but it's the hardest thing there is to learn—is just to relax a little."

"You relate everything to judo, don't you?"

The Judoka grins and nods. "Yes, I suppose I overdo that. Judo, like all systems, is incomplete; one has to make exceptions to it. But judo is more than people usually think. It's what the Orientals call a Way, a sort of path through the water. The fighting method is central to it, but it's not the whole thing."

Then the young woman, suddenly quite intent, asks the man if he does not get rather lonely out here by himself.

The expression on the Judoka's face fades and becomes only a slight, sad half smile. "Yes," he says. "Not often. Most of the time I am quite content with sea and wind and books. Also, I'm with people quite a bit. Still, there are times when I get lonely." The smile brightens slightly, but somehow becomes even sadder. "Usually when it happens, I feel just a little melancholy, the way you do when you're in a strange city and the lights begin to go on in people's windows. But that pensive feeling is rather pleasant—it's the appropriate mood for dusk."

But now the Judoka's expression changes again. Now the sadness is more profound than any the young woman has known; mingled with it is a touch of sheer horror. Leeda is sorry she asked the question; her eyes are smoky. The man continues: "There are other times when I am really alone . . . so alone it's—I can't say . . . I wouldn't like you to see me then . . . but I'll tell you about that sometime when I know you better."

Leeda is relieved at the breaking off of the subject, yet now she is not sorry that she has asked the question. For an instant, she feels, the Judoka's soul has been as bare as his body was this morning, and she knows him more completely for it.

She shifts her legs and stands up. "When are you going to start teaching me judo?" she asks.

"I'm already teaching you," the Judoka replies, grinning again. "Everything I do is judo—or, at least, I intend it to be.

The woman smiles and nods. Her eyes brighten; the Judoka notices that she is one of those rare people whose eyes really do that.

"However," he says, "we will take up the fighting art. Let's take a walk and a swim first."

A short while later they are on a stretch of level and fairly firm sand a few feet from the enclosure The Judoka begins the workout by stretching: back bent backward as far as it will go, then forward until the head touches the knees, then head to knees while sitting. Leeda does all of these as fully as the Judoka and even more gracefully. "Maybe you should be teaching me," he says; but then he goes into a headstand from which he pushes up into a handstand, a feat the girl cannot duplicate.

"I notice that you maintain normal breathing while holding the postures," he says. "I had to work at that for a good while and read about the yogis doing it."

"One other yogic notion—" he starts.

"Yes?"

"Well, it sounds kind of silly. The yogis have an idea that while holding these postures you should be conscious of taking *prana*—life, I guess you'd say—into your person and of expelling used prana, now poisonous. Just what that kind of imagining does I don't know, but unless I'm fooling myself it makes the exercise *feel* or *seem* more valuable. Anyway, it's an idea." He shrugs.

Next the Judoka takes up the moving postures, "loosening up" by touching toes, shaking the hands freely, rotating the neck and back and ankles. The dancer uses some of her own routines for this purpose.

Now the Judoka moves over a few paces and draws with his toe a fifteen-foot square. This square, he says, is the mat of the dojo and is to be regarded as such. He shows his pupil how to bow from the waist as she steps onto or off the mat. He points out that this ceremony is rigidly observed by judomen everywhere.

For a moment Leeda loses herself in a reflection on this bit of rigidity at the heart of what she already understands to be one of the most flexible of Ways—as if the two qualities must achieve some kind of balance.

The first art of judo, the man says, is *ukemi*—ways of falling without hurting oneself, often called breakfalls. "But I guess dancers study how to fall?"

"Well, a little, in gymnastic work. But it's been a while since I've done any of that."

The Judoka nods and has her sit with her legs stretched out in front of her and her arms paralleling them. Now just fall back, he says.

She does, and hits the ground with only a slight jar. She grimaces. "It's been a while, I guess," she says.

"You didn't do badly. Your back was just a little too straight. Tuck your chin into your neck and make your back round. The idea is to make a wheel of your back so that you don't make impact with the whole thing at once."

Soon the young woman is rolling back smoothly. Next the Judoka has her lie on the ground on her back and slap the ground with both hands. smacking sharply until the hands almost bounce back up on their own. When she has learned this, the Judoka has her sit up again and fall, now slapping the ground as she falls. The idea, he explains, is to take advantage of the principle that every action has an equal and opposite reaction: the hands induce a reaction that softens the impact on the back. It is a kind of judo of falling, he adds; rather than blocking the fall, one goes with it, taking it even a bit harder than necessary with a part of the body that is fairly tough.

Next, he has her squat and fall back. The slap should start at the instant you feel the ground touch your backside, he says. He shows her how to fall with one foot slightly behind the other so that she can be ready either to fend off an adversary, should that be desirable, or to get up quickly.

When she can do the falls fairly well, he has her stand up and fall back, going through the squatting posture without pausing in it. Then he teaches her to squat and fall off to each side and then to stand and fall off to each side. Not being accustomed to much impact, she is now sore and tired. To give her some relief, the Judoka starts going in the other direction: he shows her a forward roll, a kind of somersault off one shoulder broken at the end by a slap. The girl has no difficulty in learning this maneuver. She does have trouble making herself yell *Kia!* as she goes into the roll, but the Judoka insists that this loud belly cry is essential. He grins and she keeps trying.

"Now I want to experiment with a little exercise I dreamed up but haven't had a chance to try out," the Judoka says. "The main trick of judo is to let the other fellow do what he wants to do, to go along with him but do it faster and further than he has counted on—go the second mile, but go it running—and carry him along with you. Now for the exercise: Close your eyes. Take my hands in yours. When you feel me push with either hand, you pull. When you feel me pull, you push. Do it as if you were dancing with me, so that it is not a matter of my push and your pull, but of a push-pull conducted by us jointly as one motion."

Leeda performs much more smoothly and easily than the Judoka has expected her to. He tells her so.

She laughs softly. "A woman has a good many disadvantages imposed on her by our culture, but she has a few advantages too. This exercise is a great deal like ballroom dancing, and I'll bet I've done a lot more following than you have."

The Judoka chuckles and then gazes for a minute out toward the sea. "You know, that's right, although I'm not quite sure what's natural and what's cultural in these affairs . . . We usually think of judo as a masculine art because we usually picture fighters as men; but actually, in its essence, judo is a feminine art.

"Well," he continues, "that's enough philosophy for the moment. Let's go back to work." He modifies the maneuver: "Occasionally I will push against one of your ankles with the sole of my foot, either from the outside or the inside. Do the same thing you do with your hands: move the foot in the direction of my push."

At first Leeda is awkward in responding to this kind of pressure on her ankles, but she soon masters the situation. She decides that judo may be fun after all.

"Open your eyes," the Judoka says. "We'll go ahead with the exercise, but in a minute I'm going to do something different. Don't freeze up. Just do exactly what you've been doing."

They go on doing the exercise until Leeda is again relaxed. Then the Judoka pulls her right hand, keeps pulling forward and up, releases her left hand and encircles her waist, steps in and turns, bending his knees and throwing his hips square into her midsection—all in one sweeping motion. Without pausing at any point, he lifts her off the ground and pitches her over onto it, not roughly but not very gently either.

"That was *o-goshi*," he says. "Major hip throw."

He shows the woman how to do it and has her "fit it" to him—do everything but lift—many times to each side. She knows that she has strong legs, but the Judoka is a big, heavily muscled man, and she is not confident that she can lift him. Nevertheless, when she is smooth in the maneuver and is making proper use of his kuzushi and has her legs under her so that she can get their full power, the Judoka tells her to lift and throw. She does. She is pleased to find that she can do it gracefully. Her instructor is not at all surprised.

"Fine," he says. "Now try it to the other side."

The shifting of sides is awkward, but he keeps her practicing until she is smooth and then until she can no longer lift him. "Now, so that you can rest, I'll throw you a few times," he says. Before Leeda can protest, she is in the air.

The Judoka throws her, using the o-goshi, several times, and then has her throw him a few more times. "That's enough," he says when she is again too tired to throw. "How about a swim, and then we'll walk down to the hotel and get something cold to drink."

"Great!" she says.

As she runs off the "mat," he calls her back to bow.

狩

There is some question as to whether or not any one person can teach another anything. There is an even more serious question about whether or not he has a *right* to do so, even if he can. For anyone is liable to be in error about "truth" and may, therefore, be teaching what is incorrect; it may be that the student would be better off without his lessons. With judo, this is certainly the case: in judo, everything—including technique—is a function of attitude, and there is some chance that the student has naturally a "better" (i.e., more effective) attitude than the instructor has developed. However, there seems to be value in people coming together in order to pursue truth, and very often one needs to direct the study and show the other what seems to work for him. But the professor should always be ready to find his ways improved upon by the student. Perhaps teaching is justified only when it is truly a hunt for truth conducted jointly by professor and student.

"All men are created equal" goes the expression, and it may be more nearly true than we sometimes think. I suspect that men have very similar *total* strength, but that one man is more highly developed in some respects while another is more highly developed in others, and that those whom we call strong men are simply those who have strengths in the particular aspects that are useful in our culture. I suspect too that each man is a microcosm who cannot really increase his total strength or decrease it except as he makes a natural arc from womb to grave, and that whenever a man develops some outstanding strength in any aspect of his being he draws that strength from elsewhere in his being, leaving him weaker there. So it is that great men, like gods, have clay feet.

The Judoka is no exception to this rule. His aloneness, which is far more profound than just not being with crowds of people, is one of his weaknesses, one of the prices he pays for his way of living.

As the Judoka tells Leeda, he is already teaching her judo as he hunts and eats. When he makes the transition to the more violent fighting art, he does it gradually and as naturally as possible, starting by stretching and then loosening up, activities of value in their own right that might be preliminary to many kinds of action other than fighting.

For his stretches, the Judoka uses those of hatha yoga, modified as he finds desirable, since that is the most thorough system of deep stretches with which he is familiar. He makes use of the yogic practice of being conscious, while holding each stretch, of drawing in strength from the outer world and expelling from himself whatever he no longer needs. This practice involves no departure from the factual nature of the situation (although he may be drawing in some things that he does not need and expelling some that he could still use) and so it is not self-deception. The yogis, as well as aikidomen (practitioners of *aikido*, an art similar to judo), feel that a consciousness of the flow of life is of value, and both the yogis and the aikidomen are able to do remarkable things with their bodies. The relations of mind to body—if there is any sense in which they are separate things—are not easy to understand; perhaps only by trying to relate them in various ways can we ever come closer to understanding them.

In order to loosen up, the Judoka makes use of calisthenics-stretches with movement—but he uses them lightly and rather playfully so that they are fun rather than drudgery. Often he varies his approach to loosening up, using games or tree-climbing or, as he does here, swimming and walking.

The insistence on ceremony as seen in the bowing is universal among judomen, and it seems to maintain in the art a spirit higher than those of some arts (and especially fighting arts) that neglect ritual. The Judoka's push-pull dance is his own invention, but it is perhaps not dissimilar to exercises conducted in many dojos. The Judoka does vary from usual American dojo practice in two ways that are really one: He puts no time limit on the session, but works with people until they are tired and then some, and he does not specify that practice throws are to be done a set number of times. He feels that awareness of number in either case is likely to distract attention from the business at hand and to make the practice a thing to be "gotten through" rather than enjoyed. He admits that the pleasure may be at times mixed with pain.

All judo instruction begins with ukemi. They are methods of falling as painlessly as possible and doing as little damage as possible. One falls by means of a circular movement, as one does almost everything in judo. The chin is tucked into the neck—it is kept that way in judo, partially as a defense against chokes—in order to avoid hitting the head or snapping the neck, but also in order to produce a vertical curve in the spine when falling. To fall with the back straight is to make impact over the whole surface at once, jarring the person and maybe even impairing for a few seconds his ability to maneuver. To fall more or less in a ball is no doubt to take more impact on each point along the circumference of the circle, but it is also to permit each point to slide off and thus be relieved at the very moment of impact. There is therefore less jar and less damage. In order to reduce the impact on the back, the Judoka slaps the mat or the ground a split second before his back begins its roll.

Koichi Tohei in his books on aikido argues against this slapping in favor of learning to fall lightly. He says that while the slap is fine on a mat, it may be disadvantageous to slap when fighting on a hard surface where one might impair his ability to fight precisely by hurting his hand. Tohei is probably right, but I think the slapping worth learning both because it may at times be useful and because it can assist one in learning to fall lightly.

Just what physical principle is called into play in falling lightly I do not know, any more than I know how a person can by exercise of his will vary his condition from that of dead weight to one that is conducive to easy carrying. But I do think it possible to learn to fall lightly, and I do think that there is a real "physical" difference in falling lightly and falling heavily. If one drops a dead cat, it falls with a duller thud than a living cat—but why, I don't know. It may be that in this matter more obviously than in any other aspect of judo the influence of attitude on bodily movement is to be seen.

Ukemi is always taught aspiring judoka, not only to help them avoid getting hurt, but to eliminate or at least reduce their fear of falling. One certainly cannot play judo at all well while in the grip of a deep dread of being thrown. A judoman in that condition would have as much chance of success as a baseball pitcher told that he must throw through the strike zone but that his life depends on no batter making contact with the ball. A judo student with a serious fear of falling would distort all of his training techniques: everything he learned would be wrong. Since ukemi is of such primary importance, the judo instructor has little choice but to take it up first.

Getting rid of the fear of falling is one aspect of a more far-reaching necessity—eliminating the ego. The image that comes to mind when one hears one's name called is not entirely without value; like everything else it has functions to perform. It is an essential factor in ambition, which provides the motivation for learning judo and for doing much else. It serves as a reference point without which we could not contemplate ourselves and our relationship with the world. It provides us with a sense of separateness without which there could be no love, for there can be no union without disunion. As long as the ego is recognized for what it is and used appropriately, it is a valuable part of the person. But it easily becomes a superstition, an idol, and when this happens it interferes with attitude. Because it is common, indeed almost universal, for the ego to be an idol (even for people who recognize intellectually that it should not be), we usually speak of the necessity of losing ego rather than speaking, more accurately, of the necessity of losing ego-as-superstition. (By *idol* I mean anything to which one clings as an absolute necessity. All idols are superstitions, for nothing recognized for what it is can be clung to as an absolute necessity. This includes the principle I have just announced.)

The ego is a fiction and, unless recognized as a fiction, an illusion. A photograph is an attempt to freeze reality, to catch it in an unchanging medium; but a photograph of a person is always out of date by the time it is developed, even if the developing takes place in a few seconds within the camera, for a person is in a constant state of change. So it is with the picture on the mind's-eye screen. That picture is distorted not only as the photograph is, but also by a person's misunderstanding of himself—his overrating of some characteristics and underrating of others. Despite these shortcomings, the ego can still be useful if recognized as a fictional approximation of what is.

Detrimental effects of ego are usually results of its illusory nature and its idolatrous status. One tries to maintain its status quo or to improve over-all the person to which it refers—both quite impossible of attainment. The ego tends to carry a person into the abstract world of the future, causing him to picture future states of failure or success, of pain or pleasure. In judo, as the fear of falling or defeat makes one too inclined to hold off the adversary to be effective, anticipation of success may make one too aggressive, too inclined to force the action and make it go in the direction one desires, to be effective. Whether the anticipation is of victory or defeat, the person is abstracted from the here-and-now reality and attention is distracted from the adversary.

So it is that the Zen swordsman Yagyū says, in Suzuki's translation, "Turn yourself into a doll made of wood: it has no ego, it thinks nothing; and let the body and limbs work themselves out in accordance with the discipline they have undergone. This is the way to win." Suzuki translates Yagyū's teacher, Takuan, as writing: "The art of the sword, as I see it, consists in not vying for victory, not testing strength, not moving one step forward or backward; it consists in your not seeing me and my not seeing you." Suzuki explains that Takuan's idea "is that the combatant is not to cherish any thought of self and no-self, for when this thought is present in his mind, his moves invite opposition and obstruction everywhere and the combat will surely end in his own ruination." In these remarks there are references to the related but different matter of no-mind, but the remarks also amount to the doctrine that a man must lose his life in order to save it. This has been the advice of sages from Jesus and Buddha down.

Sacrifice of the ego is not easy. One can superficially imagine doing it easily, but a crisis is likely to jar one back into the habitual attitude. It is frightening to let go of the self—as frightening as death, for that anticipated loss is what creates the fear of death.

One learns to sacrifice the ego in part by adopting a philosophy that reveals the fictitious nature of the ego and the value to be derived from recognition of that nature. Prior to or during a fight, one loses ego, as we saw the Judoka do it by means of fear and love. But perhaps the most effective way to dispose of the ego problem is by means of still another form of judo: Norman O. Brown has suggested that death is an enemy because we have too much unlived life within us. Perhaps, then, we can best escape excessive fear of annihilation by being as fully alive as possible all of the time—by not putting off life.

道場

# MAKING

Leeda arrives at the Judoka's enclosure the next day, it is nearly noon. She has spent the morning collecting shells, she says, holding open a small bag for his inspection.

"I felt like working—if you can call it that—this morning," she says, "and after I got started I forgot about time."

"Do you suppose it's possible that the only kind of work worth doing is that which makes one ask that question and lose oneself in it?" the Judoka replies. He adds that he is in much the same situation and asks if she is now in a hurry. She answers that she is not and that she would be pleased to sit and do nothing for a while.

The Judoka is making a fishnet. Leeda asks why he needs more fishnets when he seems to have several already. He chuckles and says that he needs this one for exactly the same reasons that she needed more seashells. He doesn't need this one to use but to sell. He wants a little money, he says, and he feels like making something with his hands; since he enjoys working with string and cord, the net-making appeals to him.

After this explanation the Judoka falls silent almost as he did while eating. The girl watches as he pulls and knots the string. She notices that he handles the string much as he handles food—almost caressing it, yet with a caress that is a curious blend of gentleness and toughness.

Despite his toughness, the Judoka forms the knots without ever forcing anything. He appears to let the string curve however it will, go around one way or another according to the lay of the fibers. Yet without interruption he completes his knots time after time.

Now Leeda observes something very strange—obviously a trick of mind and eye, she thinks, no doubt a measure of her infatuation with this man: As the net forms, it seems to take on, whether physically or not it is hard to say, the very personality and character of the Judoka himself. The illusion makes the young woman angry because she thinks she is being childish. She shakes her head and blinks rapidly, but the phenomenon will not go away. Finally, she smiles. If she is going insane, the process has about it a little of the feel of entering a fairy-tale world.

Abruptly the Judoka lays the net aside and rises. Leeda is disappointed: she wants to see how the net is going to "come out," as if it were a story.

"Aren't you going to finish it?" she asks.

"I don't especially want to finish it," he says. "Sometime I will. Let's go play some judo."

He takes her out on the sand. After stretching and loosening up, they review the various ukemi, the push-pull dance exercise, and the o-goshi. Then he shows her a new throw, *o-soto-gari*, to be used when the adversary is pulling her. He teaches her to step up quickly, place her hip alongside his, and then swing her inside leg quickly forward and then backward and against his leg while simultaneously shoving against his shoulders. This is an easier throw than the o-goshi, but for that very reason a judo student is likely to try to force an opportunity for it. The Judoka cautions his pupil against this, and then has her practice this throw alternately to each side and alternately with the o-goshi until she is exhausted. They bow to each other and bow again at the edge of the "mat" and return to the enclosure.

"Now I'm the one who feels like doing nothing," the Judoka says. "I mean literally nothing, or as near nothing as possible. I don't want to work or visit or talk or walk or play or even rest. I'm not tired. It's just that doing nothing is what I want to do—if that makes sense, which it doesn't. But I'd hate your leaving."

Leeda is delighted. This is the first time he has said anything about enjoying her presence, although he has shown that he does. She would feel even more highly complimented if she knew how rarely he finds himself torn between two desires—trying to go two ways at once or to hold on to anything.

"Maybe I can stay around and read or just look at the ocean," she says.

"Good," he replies.

She takes the copy of *Moby Dick* from the crate, but Melville's cetology seems too ponderous for her mood. She returns it and takes the only other book, a volume of essays by the airy saint-Exupéry. She settles down to read.

The Judoka sits in what the yogis call the hero's posture: on the ground, with one foot resting on the other thigh. His back is straight, and he looks out over the sea. For a while he has a few wandering thoughts, but he sets these aside gently but deliberately. Then he sinks into—or rises into, the sensation is of sinking and rising at the same time—a condition similar to no-mind but differing from it in that he is more than usually aware of himself as being in the condition. Yet the "himself" of which he is aware continually varies in form: at one extreme of this variation "himself" seems pure void, a nothingness pervaded by the sand, sea, and sky around him, but a void that is alive in its nothingness; at the other extreme "himself" is everything—the sand, sea, and sky are simply his being, just as his hand is. At one point, a thought obtrudes: he could, if he wished, stop or divert the swoop of the seagull at the water's edge in exactly the same way that he could stop or divert a sweep of his own arm; he is tempted to do it.

After a while, he grows fidgety, but this very tendency of his body to move for no reason and to no end seems a part of himself, and he smiles as he recognizes in his movements a portrait of himself with emphasis on his weaknesses. He shifts out of the hero's posture into the judo kneeling position, the one in which he reads. This major movement takes care of his need to move, and now he sinks (or rises) further. Now "himself" is neither void nor everything, it simply is. It is at once a unity and a diversity, an incarnate harmony. It is neither more nor less than simple vitality, but in being that it is all and nothing.

道
場

It is possible that a person should restrict himself in general to those kinds of work into which he can enter as adventures into a medium. For a person who can act in this way, there is no sacrifice of part of the life for "goods" to be enjoyed during "leisure" time—instead, there is work which is of value even if nothing is gained in exchange and even if there is no achievement recognizable as a product. In addition, the person who works in this way is likely to do better work than the person who does not, to achieve a product of better quality, and consequently very often to gain more in exchange. More important, the person who regards the day as an opportunity to do what he wants to do is better off per se than the person who regards the day as a unit into which he must fit the various kinds of work required of him. The difference is vast, and far more of us fall into the latter category than the former. To move from the latter category into the former is to regain something like a child's view of the world and to engage in what Thoreau called the highest of arts, that of affecting the very quality of the day.

Hunting is an enterprise man shares with the animals. Making, other than the making birds do of their nests and beavers do of their dams, is a more distinctively human undertaking. A man makes use of what others have made— sits in a chair, sails a boat, or reads a book—and then he himself wants to make. It is a cycle. Man has a creative urge. Coleridge says that one kind of making, writing, is a form of divine analogy and that it raises a man closest to the stature of the gods. I think that may be true of other kinds of making as well.

Making is a judo in which the adversary is the medium in which one works. It must be remembered, however, that making, like fighting or hunting, is successful only when one loves the adversary. Genuine making requires close and sympathetic attention to the medium and primary attention to the means rather than the end. It also requires letting the medium express itself, which is why we see the Judoka letting his string suggest its own turns. One can best see how this works with respect to a fine art like sculpture. A true sculptor does not often just think up a subject (except in a broad sense) and go out and find a rock upon which he can impose it. Rather, he sees a rock that suggests to him a subject or a treatment of a subject, and then he tries to draw that work of art from the rock. (In fact, both the sculptor and the rock determine the treatment, just as both the Judoka and his adversary determine the pattern of throws.) While this relation between worker and medium is more obviously necessary in sculpture than in net-making, it is necessary to real craftsmanship in doing anything.

The only really worthwhile objects are those that are crafted individually by a person who loves his task. It would seem that a maker of machine tools who loved those machine tools could create one that would then stamp out valuable objects in mass production; but this does not seem to work. Apparently human love cannot be passed on to a second stage in this fashion. At best only part of the spirit passes down.

Just why this individual-craftsmanship-in-love is necessary is hard to say. The people who make wooden desks have a slogan that goes, "If you're not working over wood, you're overworking." Their argument is that the grain of the wood, being irregular, provides a less monotonous and consequently less tiring working surface than does steel. It may be that individually made things, especially when the media have been permitted to express themselves, have the same irregularity in natural rhythm that makes natural objects interesting and pleasing. The difference in atmosphere between a neighborhood of old carpenter-built houses and a housing development of partial pre-fabs suggests what I mean.

It may be too that the matter of an object is imbued with the spirit of the creator. This is what I think to be the case, but since I can hardly expect that explanation to be taken at face value by many readers, I will try to explain in more mechanistic or analogical terms.

Let's take the writing of a novel, which corresponds to the building of anything else, the process being the selecting and assembling of words. In his Experiment in Criticism C. S. Lewis suggests that every serious writer breathes into whatever story he tells all of the wisdom he has. A little reflection shows that this is not just a possibility: it is *necessarily* what happens. A novelist creates a character and puts her (say) in a critical circumstance. Now the novelist (if he is serious—that is, not writing according to formula) loses a major part of his conscious control of the action. The character takes over and responds to the circumstances as she, her kind of person, has to respond to them. Events follow as they must. But all of this response and causal is conditioned and determined by the way in which the novelist thinks the world works. It cannot be any other way if the novelist is serious. Thus his wisdom—or his lack of it—is breathed into the story. Since each "part" of his wisdom is conditioned and shaped by all the other "parts," even a plot of narrow scope is going to reflect all of his wisdom.

That the artist's wisdom is a component part of his novel is easy to see. It is not too difficult to see in the case of a musical composition or a sculpture or a painting. It is more difficult to see, but I think the principle still holds, in a case in which the artist works in the useful arts—making chairs or dresses or fishnets.

Perhaps one of the aspects of the individually made item that we like is its uniqueness, its originality. If everything around us were "standard" and mass-produced, the world would look like a contemporary motel room. If everything were unique, it would resemble a forest. The difference between the two is awesome.

Originality too is the result of a kind of judo. Originality is easy to achieve; it requires not genius but honesty. If my fingerprints are unique, then surely so is my *Weltanschauung*—my world view, the whole set of ideas and attitudes and perceptions and conceptions and interpretations that makes up "me." All I have to do to be original is to look at anything—judo or seahunting or net-making or man-meets-woman or what have you—and let what I see pass through the filter of my *Weltanschauung*, which will impress its shape upon the material, and then let emerge an honest report of what happens. Since my Weltanschauung is as unique as my fingerprints, and since it is going to shape the material and all interpretations of it, what emerges—if I can let it come out honestly—has to be unique, original.

But this is not to say that what emerges has to be valuable. This is where the genius comes in. Given originality, value derives from the depth and consistency and poetic quality of the *Weltanschauung*. These qualities may depend on perceptiveness and other factors and may not be so readily gained. But any person can be original.

However, even just being original is not quite as easy as it should be because most of us have forgotten how to be honest. No matter how honest we are, we cannot really see "what is there" because our culture and our language teach us to divide things and set up boundaries in certain ways and so to categorize what we see; it probably does take genius to get beyond this barrier. But most of us do not even get as close as we might. By habit—which is a necessary but easy-to-overuse device for reducing the challenge of the world and making it easier to cope with—we see less than we might, or see less accurately than we might, and think and report less honestly than we might. We train ourselves (unknowingly, of course) to read into events the lessons we think we are supposed to learn from them, and we habitually think what we believe we are supposed to think. Honesty requires a close and sympathetic attention to what is, an egolessness—a putting ego out of the way so that report is not colored by extraneous considerations—and a yielding to what is; thus a kind of judo.

All objects vary in effect according to the thought and experience of the viewers. That is to say, every man brings himself in all of his aspects to whatever work of art he views or object he uses; and what he gets from the work of art or the object is determined by what he is when he comes to it. (For example, an adult reader of a good children's story gets something quite different from it than does a child.) But only the object made wisely, only the object made with love, permits him to immerse himself fully in it and thus get back full measure for what he brings.

Any object made with love, any object made well, contributes to making the world poetic—to making it mythic, to making it enchanted, to making it worth living in.

And so does the process of making it, the means as well as the end, contribute to making the world poetic. And so does a service as well as a product—the Judoka's judo instructing and hunting as well as his net-making.

He who contributes to making the world poetic is a poet. The man who writes verse may work in the most difficult medium, and a single product of his endeavor may do more to render the world worth living in than the single product of another man's, but he does not stand alone as a poet. The maker of good fishnets or judo lessons is also a poet.

The Judoka, as a man who practices a peculiarly poetic Way in all that he does, is in a better position than most people to function as what I would call *the True Poet*. The ideal of this speculative character has somehow formed in my mind on the model of King David and a fictional counterpart of his, Tolkien's Aragorn.

David was a poet, the writer of the Psalms. He was a fighter, of Goliath and Saul, and a lover, of Bathsheeba. He was a shepherd rather than a hunter, but his shepherding (which itself was a way of "finding" food) seems to have involved considerable slingshot-hunting. He was a healer who soothed Saul with music and oil, a teacher who instructed his people in the ways of God, and a statesman who united his people.

Aragorn is a character in Tolkien's mythic *Lord of the Rings*. He too is a poet, mostly as a storyteller and as one who assists others in the composition of song. He too is a fighter; it is he who generals the battle against the dark lord. He too is a lover, of an elvish princess. We first see him as

Strider, a Ranger who forages for his food and who is competent in the preparation and application of medicinal herbs. Later we see him as the guide (i.e. teacher) of the fellowship of the ring. Finally, we see him as the king whose coming has been prophesied. One of his first acts as king is healing by the laying on of hands.

There can be little doubt that the current world needs true poets as badly as did that of the days of David or that of the fictional dark days of Middle Earth. The point seems hardly worth making in our motel-modern, fragmented, standaridized, despairing world, which lacks so much faith, hope, and love.

It seems to me that the True Poet—the man who can be of most assistance in making the world poetic—can function in at least four ways that are kinds of making. These four functions are in addition to the primary ones of fighting, loving and hunting. I see them as activities of the Judoka because I think of judo as a poetic way.

The Judoka or True Poet is maker, healer, teacher, and king. As poet or maker (the Greek word from which we get "poet" means "maker") he may make or do anything—judo, like dance, is an art as surely as the writing of verse or the tying of fishnets—as long as he makes or does it well, with love. A healer is also a maker, working in the far more complex medium of the human being. His making in this instance is not creation—it really isn't in any instance—but freeing of the medium (i.e., the patient) to express himself and develop as he will. The same is true of the teacher, who is doing exactly the same thing as the healer except that whereas *therapy* attempts to enable the *patient* to get himself into "normal" range, *education* tries to help the *student* raise himself above it. The king is only a manager, but that "only" is not derogatory. The manager, the true manager, is healer and teacher of those who work for him, for the primary purpose of any organization is to facilitate the growth and life of the people who compose it; and he is a maker whose task is too great or too complex for one man to accomplish and so requires organization. The actual king or statesman is a manager of managers whose product is the proper conduct of the primary human functions of hunting, fighting, and loving. And so we come around full circle.

After working at the fishnet and making a judo lesson, the Judoka engages in a making of nothingness. He sits quietly, doing nothing. Paradoxically, this is the hardest work of all.

For most of us it would be far harder than it is for the Judoka. If you don't believe me, try it. Just sit, with your back straight, concentrating "but not in your thoughts" as the Zen masters say, literally doing virtually nothing. It is hard for most of us for several reasons. One is that we do not usually get enough exercise for our whole bodies, and therefore parts of our bodies are always needing exercise rather than relaxation—and so we fidget even when we try to relax. (The Judoka overcomes this difficulty by exercising before he even tries "just sitting." In this instance, he has just completed a judo session; one of the values of judo, as of hunting, is that it involves the entire body, and a healthy person wants from time to time activity into which he can throw his whole person. When the Judoka wants to meditate or just sit but he has not recently engaged in whole-person exercise, he does a few yoga stretches.) Another is that sitting quietly, doing nothing, is an unaccustomed activity for us, and so throws us into an unknown world. Still another is that sitting quietly, doing nothing seems to us a waste of time.

Yet it is far from being a waste of time. It is a making as truly as the weaving of the fishnet is. This contention makes sense when one realizes that the primary "product"—the most important one—of any making process or any other kind of work is not the thing made or the job completed but the full life of the maker or worker.

Just sitting is the making of a self-portrait. It is precisely because one comes to know oneself in a new way by sitting quietly, doing nothing, that this "activity" is actually frightening to most of us. The very movements we make in fidgeting, the temptations to stop and engage in other activities, the fears of not being at all that arise while doing nothing—all of these figure in the portrait; and if the Gestalt Therapists are right (that awareness itself is therapeutic) the portrait can be of assistance in developing the person.

More importantly, sitting quietly and doing nothing is a state of being in itself. But, like other things that are of value in and for themselves (education, for example) it has by-product value. Sitting quietly, doing nothing, very often produces in the person—after he passes the stage of anxiety—great vitality and a feeling of harmony with the world. Thus, the activity provides the necessary relaxation for the rhythmic contraction required in other making.

道
場

The next day Leeda arrives early at the Judoka's enclosure and again hunts and breakfasts with him. On this occasion she is more helpful than before as hunter. Afterwards they talk, walk, and swim, and then he gives her a third judo lesson, this time adding *tai-otoshi*, body-drop, a forward-kuzushi throw executed by hopping around to the side of the adversary, low, with a leg in front of him, and then twisting him over the leg. To this the Judoka adds a few hold-downs and shows his pupil some tactics to use when both fighters are off their feet.

Later he invites her to go with him on an unusual project. A few weeks before, a mother, having read his notice at the hotel, brought to him her twelve-year-old son who suffers from asthma. She said that she had taken the boy to various physicians and clinics without success and that she was now desperate. She wondered if exercise might help.

"I am giving him judo lessons," the Judoka says, "although I'm going very slowly. The boy has been coming twice a week for four weeks, and he's about where you were at the end of your first lesson. I'm also having him walk out here for his lessons—his mother wanted to bring him by car—and take a walk along the beach every morning and afternoon. But now and then I add a little therapy of my own. I don't call it that because his mother would be skeptical, but that's what it is. I like to do it at his house."

The Judoka and the young woman walk down the beach to town, she in her yellow bathing suit again. The town is little more than a village, and the house is but a few blocks inland from the hotel. It is a small, white house in the middle of a block, without much shrubbery, dwarfed yet protected by more imposing houses on either side.

The mother greets the Judoka and his companion at the door with a nervous welcoming smile. The front room is dark, the walls dominated by religious symbols of ornate design. The atmosphere is close despite an air conditioner. Leeda draws in her shoulders and wonders how a man who lives outdoors can even breathe in this room, but when she looks at the Judoka he does not appear to be bothered; indeed, as he walks through the house it is the house and not the Judoka that seems to be affected.

The boy's room is a bit brighter than the front room. The boy is putting together a puzzle at a card table in a corner. He is a rather small boy for his age, pale and thin, but with a good frame. As the Judoka walks in, Leeda sees the small boy's apathetic eyes take on, if not vitality, at least a little excitement.

Both Leeda and the Judoka sit down, and the mother leaves the room, shutting the door. The boy shows his visitors what he is doing with his puzzle, and then he describes a television drama he watched last night. The Judoka asks several questions. Leeda smiles pleasantly despite her complete lack of interest in the subject, but then she notices that the Judoka's conversation has about it nothing of the manner of an adult with a child or of the bedside manner of the physician. He continues to ask questions and to comment on the drama until Leeda begins to wonder if this man is naive enough to take seriously a run-of-the-mill TV series. Surely not, she thinks. Still . . .

When the Judoka describes the girl's shell-collecting and his own fight, he seems to delight so much in the telling that Leeda almost wonders if he has come here to help the boy or to show off before him. Nonsense, she tells herself. She stops trying to analyze the man and begins to really listen. The conversation becomes more interesting.

After a while the Judoka asks the boy if he is ready for his massage.

"With her in the room?" the boy asks.

"I'd like her to see how it works, if you don't mind," the Judoka says. "You can wear a bathing suit this time."

"Okay," the boy answers, uncertainly.

When the Judoka and the woman leave the room for the boy to change, she tries to excuse herself, but he is quite insistent that she stay. They return to the room.

"Does Leeda's presence make you nervous or anxious?" the Judoka asks the boy.

The boy says nothing.

"Does your chest feel tight? . . . All right, let it be tight. Tighten it up a little more yet. Be even more anxious." The Judoka's voice is kind, but for a few moments the boy seems terrified. The Judoka takes the boy's hands and says, "We'll both tighten up and be frightened." And, to the woman's amazement, for a few seconds the Judoka's own breathing is shallow and his face takes on an anxiety to match the boy's. There seems to be no acting to this, and neither the Judoka nor the boy appears to feel that there is anything silly about what they are doing.

After what seems a long time, the boy smiles. "I'm all right now," he says.

The Judoka spreads a pallet on the floor. The bed is too soft, he explains to the girl. The boy lies on his stomach, and the Judoka begins to work on his feet. He kneads the feet, meanwhile instructing the boy to relax. Now his voice is different: it is soothing, monotonous, the voice of a hypnotist. He works his way up the boy's leg, instructing the boy to relax each portion of the leg as he goes along. He moves to the hand and arm in the same fashion, and then to the other arm and the other leg, and then to the hips, back, and neck and shoulders, always with the more vigorous stroke toward the heart. Now he goes over the same areas again, more quickly and roughly this time, instructing the boy that he is to feel life flow into him from the Judoka's hands and that he is to permit any fear and anxiety to flow out from him into the Judoka's hands. Then he has the boy turn over, and he goes through the whole process on the boy's front side.

When the Judoka and his companion leave, the boy says nothing about feeling better, but he does say, "Thanks for the visit," with obvious pleasure.

Leeda, however, is concerned. Walking to her hotel, she asks the Judoka if he really feels it best for the boy to get rid of his anxieties by pretending they are not there.

"That's not quite the idea," the Judoka replies. "One has to recognize the anxiety and let it do whatever it will, ultimately. It even helps sometimes to intensify it as we did prior to the massage. But it helps occasionally to learn what it feels like to be without anxiety."

Leeda waits for further explanation, but the Judoka offers none.

"Well, I hope your massage does him some good," she says.

"I try not to hope anything," he answers.

道
場

J apanese physicians have long prescribed training in the
martial arts as therapy, much, I suppose, as American
doctors prescribe golf or swimming. It seems to me that
there are far more possibilities than just exercise in judo as
therapy and that *kappo*—the traditional art of resuscitation
taught to judomen upon reaching the rank of first-degree
black belt—should be extended to include these.

Underlying most of what I have to say about both
education and therapy is my belief that they are identical—
that they are both simply processes of human development,
of development of the mind-body that has not reached its
highest possible state. Traditionally, we have used different
procedures to attain "therapeutic" and "educational" ends,
and perhaps there is some justification for doing so, but
there is no fundamental reason that we should have to do
so. (Since we accepted the Cartesian split of body and mind
we have centered our therapy on the body and our education
on the mind, neglecting mental health and physical
education to the detriment of both body and mind. No
doubt it is at least partially because we have believed in the
split that we have adopted different procedures—we
thought we were dealing with different kinds of things.) Yet
the processes that can do the one can also do the other.

If my belief about the relation of therapy to education
is correct, and if, as experience seems to suggest, the most
effective teaching is accomplished simply by being, it follows
that the most effective healing is accomplished by being.

To phrase the matter another way, I think that health is
contagious. There is no reason to suppose that disease is

contagious but health not. I know that disease is supposed to be transmitted by "germs," but there are also "germs" that immunize us from disease, and the physicians tell us that there has to be an external cause (the disease germs) and an internal cause (lack of resistance) for disease to occur. If the disease germs can move around, why not the resistance ones? Our popular notion that disease alone can spread probably results from the cultural assumption that health is the norm, and consequently a blank and negative sort of thing, whereas disease is a positive evil.

Whatever the theoretical explanation, I have known people whose very presence makes one feel better—and often this improved feeling is not only relief of symptom but is profoundly therapeutic—and makes one almost ashamed to be sick. Jesus has been described as having so much strength and vitality that it overflowed his person and flooded those around him. This is the effect I mean. The Judoka is a healer in this way.

This treatment-by-being is not only potentially the most efficacious of therapies but also the safest. Healing, like teaching, should not try to form a person in a mold conceived by the physician or the professor, for the physician or the professor may be wrong about what is the best mold for a particular person or for people generally. Rather, healing and teaching should try to free the person to develop according to his own nature. Healing or teaching by the simple outflow of one's own strength is less likely to generate mistakes than healing or teaching deliberately.

But we are not yet strong enough to depend on healing in this way. We must still attempt to "do" some of our healing. Judo as a poetic way of doing anything is also a poetic way of healing. The Judoka has some unique training that can be applied to the task of deliberate therapy.

Earlier in this essay I mentioned Arnold Veisser's "paradoxical theory of change," which is a judo applied to a particular kind of psychotherapeutic problem. Other Gestalt Therapists use judos to approach other psychological disorders. Perls, Hefferline, and Goodman say that guilt and resentment are often feelings generated by and in a person who stands in a *confluent* relation to another person (a relation that is neither a proper union nor a proper differentiation but one that the guilty or resentful person thinks he must maintain) when that relation is disturbed. The disturbance threatens the status quo and calls for a confrontation either to reestablish the status quo (unlikely) or to establish a new relation, either closer or more clearly differentiated. But the person usually wants to maintain the status quo without a confrontation. He feels either guilt (if he thinks himself responsible for the disturbance) or resentment (if he thinks the other party responsible). This guilt or resentment is a defense mechanism against the confrontation, *which the person realizes, consciously or subconsciously, is inevitable and necessary.* The cure is the confrontation. In other words, in many cases of guilt and resentment, the treatment may be a judo, that is, a pulling response to the push of circumstance and a going around to the back door. Perls, Hefferline, and Goodman also maintain that anxiety is caused by the blocking of excitement. Whether the excitement be caused by fear or anger or sexual desire or whatever, the shallow breathing that results from blocking it is the anxiety, they say. Their treatment is a paradoxical one: going with the disorder, deliberately constricting the chest still further, thereby causing a reaction and unblocking the anxiety. (They do not say that this treatment will cure anxiety, but they do say that it may offer the patient some relief. It seems to me likely that in the case of anxiety relief may be a step toward cure.) This treatment, too, is obviously a judo. We see the Judoka applying it to the boy.

These examples pertain to psychotherapy, but as we see in the shallow breathing of anxiety, the difference between *psycho* and *physio* may be chiefly linguistic. What is psycho-therapeutic, then, may also be physio-therapeutic, and vice versa.

Judo may be applied directly to "physical" disorders. Suzuki translates the Zen swordsman Yagyū as saying: "Let yourself go with the disease, be with it, keep company with it: this is the way to get rid of it." The concept is almost funny; imagine yourself being friendly to your next bad cold. But perhaps the humor cloaks something of value.

Probably the physician who has used a form of judo most spectacularly and most successfully against organic disease is Georg Groddeck, author of *The Book of the It*. Groddeck held that the conscious self controls but very few of a person's activities. Most of a person's activities—including not only his "voluntary" ones but those of his heart and lungs and nervous system and even those of his growth and decay—are controlled by the True Self, which Groddeck called the *It* because that was the most impersonal term available, the one most lacking in connotation and thus in implied character. (The *It* is not quite the same as Freud's unconscious: the It includes ego, superego, id, body—the whole man.) Everything that a man does is an expression of the *It*. A painting and cancer are equally expressions of the *It*. The *It* is always doing exactly what it wants to do; it cannot be forced to do anything that it does not want to do, although one of its parts, the conscious self, can alter somewhat—usually detrimentally—what would otherwise be its expression. All a healer can do is to attempt to influence a patient's *It*. Anything the healer does may or may not influence the *It* or influence it in the way the healer desires—so an old wives' remedy may do as well as sophisticated surgery, although perhaps the latter will work more often, and in an emergency one must do whatever seems most likely to be of aid. (Groddeck had little faith in scientific knowledge of causal relations; he felt that anything that could be stated would sooner or later be disproved.) Groddeck himself used massage, diet, and psychoanalysis more than he did drugs and surgery, feeling that the less radical means would work as well as the more radical.

Essentially, then, Groddeck felt that the physician's job is to serve as a catalyst for the patient's *It*, which in the course of time might be influenced to express itself less painfully.(Thus Groddeck came close to healing by simply being.) Treatments of various kinds may have some effect, but their main purpose is to keep the patient in touch with the physician.

It is in the manner whereby the physician enables himself to serve as catalyst that the judo comes in. Groddeck says that the physician must *lose his desire to heal*. According to Lawrence Durrell, who has written a fine essay on Groddeck, the latter's treatment of a disease is a kind of spiritual athletic, in which the patient tries to influence his own *It* and the doctor tries to keep himself from interfering. Not to desire to cure is not the same as to desire not to cure. The point is that the patient must be left free to develop as he will, not as the physician wants him to. A desire to "heal" a patient is a wish to change him from what he is into what he is not; that this wish is founded on widely established definitions of "sickness" and "health" makes no difference. To wish to change him into what he is not is not to love the patient at all, but to love an idealized conception of the patient. Groddeck's idea is that one can help the patient only by letting him be what he is—in other words, by loving him. The parallel between Groddeck's method and Arnold Veisser's paradoxical theory of change is evident.

Groddeck's yielding method tries to influence the *It* by creating—or rather allowing to develop—a new consciousness. This is the way he thought any therapy treats: both drugs and surgery create new consciousness. (The danger is that they may do it too radically and, unless the physician loves the patient as he is, influence the *It* at cross-purposes to its own nature and thus ultimately do more harm than good.)

Any experience changes the consciousness. Any radiant experience changes it in an aesthetically satisfying manner. According to Owen Barfield's definition, whatever changes the consciousness in an aesthetically satisfying manner is Poetry. Thus poetry—whatever is poetry to the patient—may be also a medicine and one likely to pick him up where he is (for if it does not pick him up where he is, it will not be, for him, poetry). These considerations open up possibilities of still other poetic—and therefore judo—therapies.

One of these is "poetry therapy" itself: the use of poetry, either the reading or the writing of it, for its effect on the consciousness of the patient. J. J. Leedy has edited a collection of essays on the subject of verse as medicine. Closely related to poetry therapy are music, art, play, and sport therapies. Groddeck's use of massage is a form of poetry therapy. Closely related to poetry therapy in another way, since poetry-as-verse entails precise use of language, is General Semantics, the attempt to make the world less confusing by clarifying linguistically induced misconceptions.

In John Barth's *End of the Road* there is a physician for whom everything is a therapy. His view is the quite correct one that every experience is either therapeutic or unhealthful. Most of his work is subsumed under the heading *mythotherapy*, a term I want to borrow, although I'm not certain that I use it to mean quite the same thing that Barth's physician does.

I use the word *mythotherapy* to refer to the therapeutic effect of being in, and even participating in the creation of, a mythic world or an enchanted world, one in which everything that happens has meaning, as it does in a novel—or even one in which everything is above meaning itself, one that has mood and tone like a work of art. One way to immerse oneself in such a mythic world is to read a mythic novel or otherwise appreciate (in the full sense of that word) a work of art. But this is not the only way.

The world itself—of an individual man and ultimately of collective man—can be fashioned as a work of art or, better and what must necessarily be the case, an infinite series of works of art. This is a difficult and dangerous matter. It is difficult for me to explain without seeming to counsel a shallowly optimistic and dishonest pretense that simply will not work and would be deadly if it did. It is dangerous for anyone to apply in about the same way and for the same reasons that it is dangerous for a man to learn to control his heartbeat—most of the time it will do a better job if left to itself. But anything that is potentially valuable is potentially dangerous.

Man knows very little; probably nothing in any profound sense of the word. An individual is like a man in a boat surrounded by fog: he can see only a little way into the fog and must try to make out where the river goes on the basis of the little he can see. In other terms, what one sees is distorted by being perceived through grids of language and culture that impose shapes not necessarily "there." On the basis of opinions interpreted from such perceptions, men collectively create a *Zeitgeist*, a spirit of the times. On a similar basis but modified again by the *Zeitgeist*, an individual creates a *Weltanschauung*, or World View, made up of all that he is and knows and through which he understands. If that *Weltanschauung* is mythic, the man's life is mythic; if it is not, neither is the man's life.

But the lack of knowledge is not altogether detrimental. Once we recognize it, we can see that it gives us a freedom that we lacked when we thought we knew more. In the late nineteenth and early twentieth centuries, we were affected by an intellectual movement called *realism*, which we now see was nothing but a simple-minded attempt to comprehend the world through the analogy of a machine. Darwin showed us that either God-as-Carpenter had not made the world in six days or else he had scattered around a number of fossils and other misleading clues to confuse us. Since his taking more than six days seemed to invalidate the Bible, and since, as Dorothy Sayers has pointed out, God-as-Novelist (creating his characters with ready-made histories) was unthinkable, we found ourselves in the darkness of Dover Beach. The mood of despair engendered by this superstition came to tint the *Zeitgeist*. Another superstition that "science" was fast establishing the true and ultimate nature of reality, tended to produce a standard *Weltanschauung*: each man felt that his must correspond to those of other men or he was somehow in error. But now we are becoming sophisticated enough to realize that the phrase "God is dead" is more of a comment on human use of metaphor than on metaphysical condition and that science deals not with reality but with phenomena. We are reverting, more or less, to the position of the medieval man, who knew that he didn't know anything. Not knowing anything, we have some freedom to play around with the *Weltanschauung*.

Picture the Judoka's *Weltanschauung* as a glass sphere made up of numerous panes. Through this glass he looks at and copes with the world. At his disposal are assortments of alternate panes that can be inserted into this all-around wind-shield. Had the Judoka been born forty years earlier, he probably would have laughed at these old-fashioned alternates (or curious new ones) and thought that the set of panes presently constituting his sphere was the only one that any intelligent man would think of using. But the Judoka was born a little late for that. As he now understands the situation, there is no necessary cause for him to prefer the pane in present use (in certain spots anyway) to some of the alternates available to fit that particular frame. For example, take the pane through which he regards the yogic device of maintaining a certain state of consciousness while holding a posture. Through one pane, this device appears to be nonsense; through another it appears to be quite reasonable. *And there is no compelling reason for him to think one of these panes clearer or more nearly true than the other.*

There are some panes that do seem to the Judoka to be clearer or more nearly true than the available alternates, and these he leaves in place. But there are many others like the one in the example. In these cases, the Judoka selects the pane that seems to work best for him. One criterion by which he judges panes is whether a particular one makes the world more or less satisfying or mythic. Thus he fashions his own *Weltanschauung* as something of a work of art.

It may happen that in some cases the Judoka will see that one of his mythic panes is distorting what is actually—in his best judgment—out there. When this occurs, he will without hesitation remove the pane and put in a less mythic one, if that is all he has available. Maybe, however—just maybe— it will turn out (if the world ever "turns out") that myth was the best of the panes tests and that the mythic panes were mythic precisely because they let through a little of the terror and joy that are at the heart of things.

Jeremy Bentham touched on this subject, in a much different mood and with different conclusions, in his Theory of Fictions. But Hans Vahinger, dealing with scientific theory making, gave a name to the kind of process l have in mind: The Philosophy of "As If." The Judoka, when there are no convincing reasons not to do so, lives as if the world were mythic.

Let me try once again to avert misunderstanding. I am not arguing that one can disregard what is and pretend that the world is what one would like it to be. To do this would be to fall into the error of "positive thinkers" or those who accept Christianity just in case it is true; it would also be to neglect that heroic myth of man confronting a hostile environment. The mythic world must, positively, be not entirely comfortable. I am saying that one does not know what the world is; and that only when there is no compelling reason to prefer a non-mythic view to a mythic one, a person is better off choosing the latter. I think there is more opportunity to do this and do it intelligently than is commonly supposed. Certainly a mythic world view is healthier than a non-mythic one and is just as likely to correspond to whatever absolute truth there is.

Joseph Chilton Pearce's *The Crack in the Cosmic Egg* is a powerful argument that man participates more actively and to more effect in constructing his reality than men have suspected. He asserts that on one occasion he and his wife delayed the effects of her terminal cancer by restructuring her concept of the nature of inevitability—and that they might have defeated the disease altogether had it not been for the skepticism of the "brass-tack realists" among the physicians. Nothing was proved by the delay, nor would anything have been proved by a recovery, as Pearce admits, but the assertion is provocative.

It is because of the Judoka's belief in "As If" psychotherapy that he combines hypnotherapy with his massage of the boy. Hypnotherapy can be worthless or dangerous if it is used to relieve symptoms without trying to approach causes, but so can drugs and surgery. It can be valuable when used as Pearce used it on his wife—he worked rather drastically, but he was in a critical situation—or as the Judoka uses it, to support what he is doing with massage, relieving a chronic situation temporarily so that the patient can see what the world is like when looked at differently (and so perhaps influence the patient's It) and to induce a sense of well-being that can have some of the effects of what Maslow calls *peak experience*.

Real hypnotherapy operates not on the symptoms alone, but on the attitude of the patient, for it is first and last on attitude—the whole stance toward the earth and everything on or above it—that health, like being and doing, depends. We are all hypnotized one way or another by language, culture, opinion—the whole of *Zeitgeist* and *Weltanschauung*. If I'm right in thinking that the mythic world view may be the most nearly "true" and certainly the healthiest and most valuable one, hypnosis that wipes out for a moment the prosaic superstition of a prosaic era may in fact be dehypnosis—provision of a moment of insight, an epiphany.

Jesus's ability to inspire in people an attitude of love may well be the explanation of his healing miracles. If this is the case, his healing miracles were not magic tricks to lure people to listen to his sermons but simple applications of what he was teaching: Love the Lord thy God, and love thy neighbor as thyself.

It is noteworthy that Jesus took his closest followers with him to lead an itinerant life. One breaks a habit or a mode of consciousness and then achieves a new one most easily and perhaps most thoroughly when one abandons the social structure built around oneself which supports the old consciousness. An itinerant life, then, may have therapeutic value: fewer aspects of consciousness have a chance to build support. The Judoka could probably do more for the boy if he could take him out to the enclosure, away from the nervous mother and the close, dark house, which may very well contribute to his anxiety.

道
場

On this day the young woman is wearing a green bathing suit, selected when she looked at the sea in the morning. "There is only one way to describe the color of the water today," she tells the Judoka. "There's a line in Joyce that suggests all the richness and beauty, but it's the most obscene line in English letters, obscene and sublime all at once: The Snot-Green Sea."

The day itself has a green quality, the Judoka observes. The sky shares the ocean's tint and is nearly aqua. The bushes sparkle more than usual against the white sand. He notices now that even Leeda's eyes, which he has thought of only as dark even when their darkness was bright, are in reality a dark green, flecked perhaps with dark brown or black.

The Judoka is wearing a *gi*. He hands to Leeda an extra suit that he keeps on hand for students; both jacket and pants are slightly large for her but not enough so as to be inconvenient.

They begin the day's lesson by doing ukemi. The Judoka asks Leeda to get down on all fours. Then he grasps the back of her jacket and dives over her, landing hard on the other side of her, on his back but looking around at the ground and slapping as he hits. He demonstrates four more times and then has her try. She hits very hard. She tries again from the other side and hits very hard again.

She tries a simpler fall but fails with it too. "My ukemi is worse than it was the first day!" she complains.

The Judoka has her go back to the diving fall. "Learn to do this one," he says, "and you will have no more trouble with falls of any kind." He keeps her falling until she begins to see the ground as she falls and to properly time her slaps. It takes quite a while.

Once again the Judoka makes use of the push-pull dance, and again he is impressed with the grace and fluidity of the girl in this exercise. He almost forgets that he is giving a lesson, and he lets the exercise run for a long time.

Now he takes up *randori*. By now Leeda has some mastery of three or four forward throws and two backward ones, so that she is ready for the free practice of throws in which the partners alternately try to feel kuzushi and throw against only token resistance. The Judoka wants this to be a "blind randori"—one in which both partners keep their eyes closed.

"When you operate entirely by feel, you develop more highly your sense of touch," he explains, "and even when you have your eyes open you get most of your kuzushi information by touch, not sight."

The blind randori goes well, and the Judoka compliments his student on her grace, her ability to relax when she is being thrown, and her knowledge of her few throws. He is not yet quite satisfied with her throws, however. "You must let your opponent throw himself," he insists.

"I think I know what you mean," Leeda says finally. "I do something like that with the poem when I dance . . . if you see what I mean . . . but I don't feel quite loose enough, somehow."

After a short break, the Judoka decides to teach the young woman a new technique, one that will capitalize on her dancing ability. He teaches her a foot-sweep, harai-tsurikomi-ashi, in which the sole of the foot is placed against an ankle just about to take the weight of a forward step.

It is really a tripping motion supported by a pull on the upper body. The Judoka has Leeda perform the throw many times in the classical fashion, and then, when she is doing it smoothly and without hesitation, he lets her begin to adapt it to her own style of doing things. When she has imbued it with her own personality, it is an even more beautiful throw than it is in its classical form.

The Judoka realizes that he may be letting the session run a little too long, and he asks Leeda if she wants to stop. She doesn't. Despite her bad beginning with the ukemi, she is moving well now and wants to go on.

Now the Judoka takes up the *ju-no-kata*, or Demonstration of Gentleness. He explains that this kata is a highly formalized ritual, a set of practice moves and responses performed in a rigid sequence, designed to impress upon both body and mind of the performer the principle of yielding.

"This kata illustrates and demands the peculiar set of mind and body—it's an emotional attitude really—that is essential to good judo," the Judoka says. He looks directly into the young woman's dark green eyes and adds: "There was once a master swordsman named Odagiri Ichiun, who taught his students by devoting *all* his attention to the development of attitude, none at all to the development of technique. Sometimes, especially when I see someone quite ignorant of technique get the better of a trained adversary, I am tempted to do the same thing."

But by the time the Judoka has finished this speech, his own attention has been diverted to an altogether different matter. Maybe altogether different, maybe not. He is reflecting on how very rare it is to meet a person with whom one can really communicate, as he seems to be able to do with this woman; how rare and how exceedingly valuable—how determining of attitude. He hopes that Leeda's mind remains on what he said, but he has doubts.

At first the ju-no-kata seems awkward to the dancer, and it feels unnecessarily rigid and too formal—too ceremonial and stilted—to be of value. However, when she has memorized the first several movements and their order, and when she and the Judoka have done them together often enough to cooperate smoothly, she begins to feel a slight touch of elation that carries with it further promise. The ju-no-kata begins to become a dance of thrusts and counters, throws and evasions. Nevertheless, after a while the memory work grows tedious, and the Judoka suggests postponing further work on the kata to the next lesson.

"Now I feel like dancing," Leeda says. The Judoka smiles.

To conclude for the day, the Judoka proposes randori, not blind or light this time, but hard. The woman is a bit frightened, for she knows that she is not ready for such a contest. But the Judoka insists. Immediately upon starting the Judoka throws her rather hard. But then he gives her an opening, and she takes advantage of it to throw him with a tai-otoshi. The process continues with the Judoka giving openings, but less obviously than has been his custom, and throwing her harder than has been his custom. Soon she is growing almost angry, and for her the randori takes on some of the character of shiai—actual contest.

Through her mild anger the woman realizes vaguely that the Judoka is treating her in this unusual contest much as he treated the boy in that unusual conversation. She has no attention to waste on how he is doing it, but she cannot help seeing that he too is engaged in some kind of contest—as much with himself, apparently, as with her. There is no condescending amusement on his face. While he is obviously not using all his strength or his knowledge, he is deadly serious about the contest. When finally she quits, exhausted, he is clearly tired himself.

They change into bathing suits and swim easily for a long time, and then relax on the beach in the greenness of the late afternoon. There seems to be something about the quality of this particular day that makes them stretch out all of their activities. It is dusk by the time he walks her back to the hotel. As the stars come out both the man and the woman are reminded of that first evening walk. He puts an arm around her, and they fit well and move together well.

They do not stop at the hotel. Without any discussion, they walk on past it and on past the town itself. They continue far along the quiet beach. Three or four miles out, they sit on a mound of sand half enclosed by a stand of small pines. The three-quarter moon is bright, there are no people around, and there is no sound of trucks and cars, and the surf is musical. Both the man and the woman are relaxed, but neither is tired.

"I think I would like to be paid for the judo lessons," the man says.

The young woman turns and looks at him evenly. She knows immediately and perfectly well that he has used that language precisely because he knows that she understands him at a level beyond the verbal.

"You want me to dance for you," she says.

"Is it too much of a request for the end of a strenuous day?"

"No. I would like to very much. But I must dance something special for you." She sits thoughtful for a while, and then she asks,

"Do you know Yeats's poem 'Leda and the Swan'?"

"Not really. I had heard of it enough to place the name when you first referred to it, but I don't know it."

"I have danced it alone—with no one watching, in my bedroom or in the woods—but I have never danced it for anyone. Somehow I want to dance it for you. It seems appropriate, and well—it just seems appropriate."

This woman has a prismatic quality for the Judoka in that she varies in his eyes, retaining a pattern but continually modifying it, like a painting. Rising now, in her long, flowing black hair and her green swimsuit, she is a vivacious girl preparing to perform for a friend. But then, arisen and standing above him, her face toward him and her dark green eyes on him, she is a figure of woman against a ground of salt wind and black water.

As she slowly unbuttons and unties the top of the bathing suit and drops it to the ground, she feels, despite her efforts to think of herself as an artist, very much a woman about to be explored by a lover. As she steps out of the bottom she is quivering slightly. She stands nude before the man, and the man is aware that a woman nude is vulnerability incarnate. Then Leeda gains firm control over herself and stands straighter, tall and proud, and is not at all vulnerable—she is a dancer, not a woman to be possessed.

She speaks: "Zeus came to earth in the form of a great swan and raped the beautiful Leda. She was terrified, but she had neither the knowledge nor the strength to cope with the god; she was but human. Against her helpless breast she felt the strange rhythm of this brute beast of the air—this bird that was also King of the Gods. In the midst of this terror came a shudder in the loins. . . . And from this union of woman and god came Helen of Troy and her faithless sister Clytemnestra, and through them the broken walls and burning towers of Troy and Agamemnon dead. . . . Yeats asks whether the girl put on the god's knowledge with his power before the indifferent beak could let her drop."

The woman, now strangely awesome in the bright night and framed to the sides by green trees, turns her profile to the man who is her audience and bends her back to point her breasts at the sky. She straightens and turns, and seems to hear and feel a great wind from above; then she is struck and begins to fall backward, but she does not fall. All is perfectly still.

Now she stiffens in terror, and then cringes; her torso seems to contract but her fingers spread and do not know what to do. Frozen, stiff-armed, she holds at bay for a few seconds the shadowy bird hovering over her . . .

Almost imperceptibly the Judoka nods, for he knows well how likely a victim is to make a futile attempt to hold off an attacker.

But the woman can hold no longer. She yields, and the terror engulfs her and spins her around and presses to her and pins her back again and enters her. No worst, there is none.

The woman tries to shrink from the pain, but she cannot, and a tremor passes through her body, a spasm of terror and hurt and despair.

But even as the pain destroys her there is a subtle shift in her posture and in the tone of the dance; her hands relax a little and her fingers, still vague, do not hold off so much as hold. And yet, while the shadowy bird is the victor, it is not at all clear that the human victim is a loser. Or it may be that winning and losing are not really different.

Now the Judoka smiles and nods again.

The woman's breast seems to respond to a strange music: the music of the waves, yes, but also of the salt wind and of the huge bird wings and of the bright stars and the three-quarter moon— the rhythm of a beast that is also a god. This female body is slave to all that is, and every movement is totally free. In her very submission the woman takes on the power of the god.

Suddenly the dancer shudders from the loins up and down through the person, and in that instant she is whole and holy, at one with the green-black substance of terror and joy.

Limbs flash and glisten, and the woman's body assumes a dozen positions at once obscene and sublime. She is at once Magdalen and the Virgin. She is in the myth with the god; she is the myth. And then she turns and faces the water and she is no longer a myth but a girl again and her jet-black hair streams down her back. She has known by acquaintance the divine itself, and she has little need for knowledge or power. If the god is indifferent, so is she; if the history that emerges is good or bad, they are in the end the same. But her indifference itself is holy. She has taken from the god and she has given to him. He has attacked and expressed the semen of a beast, and she has yielded and impressed the music of the spheres.

She turns and faces the Judoka, as if to say that she too knows a Way. The Judoka is reflecting that the dancer has just done for him precisely what the god did for her, and he knows that she at times attains—and can pass on to others—that mind-set that is the magic formula for doing all things.

The nude woman now returns to her ordinary identity, and although she herself is not quite ready, she wonders if the man assumes that her nakedness implies an offer of her body.

The Judoka meets her gaze and understands her. He smiles and shakes his head. "One does not lightly mount the recent favorite of a god," he says.

道
場

We do not have in the English language enough words to properly distinguish everything that is distinct. (Yet having more would aggravate our tendency to see distinction where it is misleading, so there is no way to win.) To fall hard "hurts" or "feels bad," yet not at all in the same way that a broken arm "hurts" or a nauseating odor makes one "feel bad." To sit in a too-soft chair "feels good," but not at all in the same sense that a brisk workout "feels good." Properly understood, feeling good or bad is an excellent guide as to what one should do or avoid doing; misunderstood, the converse is true.

That there is no way to win—no way to get an edge on the world, no way to always gain—is the first principle to be mastered by anyone who wants an education. The world is a seesaw, one end of which must go down if the other is to go up. Leeda must know the "pain" of awkward falls (which is still very different from the pain of real damage) if she is ever to know the satisfaction of good ukemi, which is quite real: it feels almost as good to be thrown well as it does to throw well. It is even more difficult and more important to understand that the very going up is a going down. The young woman's experience of performing her ukemi less well at a later stage in her training than she did at first is a common one in learning. As she begins to grasp the science, she loses some of her natural poetry. She will go on beyond this stage and ultimately recombine her science with her natural grace; then she will really know how to fall. But then she will have lost something else: the adventure, the thrill, of falling when she is not quite able to cope and the sensation is unusual. There is no getting around the principle. It is a difficult one to recognize, for our tradition glorifies education as altogether good.

The principle holds too with regard to what one teaches. It does not seem exaggerated to suggest that anything declared is from some point of view wrong, that everything I say in this book can be reversed and come out just as "true." For example, I have pointed out that the Judoka's always doing exactly what he wants to do is a virtue; yet at times there is also virtue in doing precisely the opposite of what one wants to do. William James has said that one can sometimes be too tired or low on energy to enter a project or to continue one, but that if one presses on it is possible to get beyond the obstacle of fatigue—get a "second wind" as we say—and tap a new level of energy. James considers this pushing of a person into higher energy levels to be a prime function of the will. It may be that real human development depends on this kind of use of the will.

Suppose yourself to be doing something and you become tired. What you want to do is rest. But if, instead of resting, you continue with what you are doing, you may get this second-wind effect, which is valuable not only insofar as it affects the completion of your project but also *in itself* and in developing your will. This would seem to invalidate the principle that one should always do what one most desires to do; yet it doesn't necessarily, for strength of will depends on strength of motive and you must have in this instance considerable desire to do what you are doing in order to push past the fatigue barrier.

So where are we? Perhaps the only thing we can say at this stage is that another point to be borne in mind by the person who wants to be educated is that there are no mechanical rules by which he can control his life. One must be like the Judoka in throwing the redhead—at once yielding to the pattern and determining it; at once playing and being played.

Subject, then, to the limitation that no statement can ever be fully true, we can look at some of the possibilities of judo as an educational art and of the judoman as teacher.

Judo is a non-verbal art and as such has potential value in a neglected area of education. Aldous Huxley, in an essay entitled "The Education of an Amphibian," shows that men live in two worlds, the verbal (in which the red light, for example, is a symbol meaning "stop") and the non-verbal (in which the light is a deep, burning scarlet modified by a shadowy checkerboard pattern), but that education is almost wholly verbal and directed toward the verbal. In cultivating one aspect of the human being while neglecting the other, we produce one-sided people who cannot really function well in either the verbal or the non-verbal world, let alone both.

Huxley proposes that we restore balance by introducing into the curricula of our schools "non-verbal humanities." These would go far beyond what we presently call "physical education" and would have as much to do with mental as with physical functions and would be especially valuable, Huxley says, in the development of creativity. Judo makes an excellent vehicle for several of the disciplines Huxley has in mind.

That sensory perception deserves as much attention in education as logic should be obvious, since all the materials for our premises come to us through the senses. Huxley lays special emphasis on the training of the kinesthetic sense, that "most fundamental of our awarenesses" upon which we depend for knowledge of how various parts of our bodies are positioned and what muscular tensions result from various physical and mental processes. Proper or improper use of this kinesthetic sense determines to a great extent proper or improper use of what Huxley calls "the psychophysical instrument"—i.e., the person, seen as mind and body working in and through each other and consequently as a unit. Among other things, the validity of thought depends on proper use of the psychophysical instrument.

Both the kinesthetic sense and the sense of touch are thoroughly exercised in the Judoka's blind randori. The sense of hearing is also exercised somewhat. In regular randori, especially immediately following blind randori, the sense of vision comes into play to an important extent. (Of course, all these senses are *used* in doing anything; but judo requires, and consequently sharpens and trains, these particular senses to function to an exceptional degree in these particular exercises.)

Misuse of the kinesthetic sense causes awkward movement, both physical and mental; conversely, consistently awkward movement corrupts the kinesthetic sense. Movement training, then, may be used to combat the deterioration in the kinesthetic sense probably caused by improper posture, too little walking, too much sitting in chairs, and so on. Dance therapy is being used for this purpose. The push-pull dance performed by the Judoka and Leeda has a different primary purpose, but it serves this one as a byproduct.

If someone charges at you from the side, and just before the impact you kneel low, he goes sprawling over your back. He can be said to throw himself. If, as he goes over, you stand up, you give him aid and make the throw a prettier and harder one. You can do much the same thing that you can by kneeling if you merely step aside (in which case you help by leaving a foot in the way) or retreat quickly (in which case you pull on his shoulders)—in other words, if you do any of the things that you would naturally do if you were not conditioned to resist and meet force with force head-on.

This is what the Judoka means in telling Leeda that she must learn to let the adversary throw himself: she must learn to take advantage of kuzushi to such a degree that she has very little left to do herself. This matter—this letting the opponent throw himself-relates to Huxley's non-verbal humanities in two ways. First, as Huxley points out, we need to *unlearn* certain bad habits of psychophysical usage. This kind of unlearning is as important an aspect of education as is the unlearning of childish superstitions. Second, as Huxley makes clear but our standard educational curriculum does not, there are many activities best performed by *not trying too hard* or even by *not trying at all*—by simply letting that part of the self beyond the conscious self take over. As Huxley puts it: "When the conscious will is used to inhibit indulgence in the bad habits which have come to seem natural, when the ego has been taught to refrain from straining every nerve, from desperately trying to 'do something,' when the personal subconscious has been induced to release its clutching tensions, the vegetative soul [i.e., the autonomic nervous system, etc.] and the intelligences which lie beyond the vegetative soul can be relied upon to perform miracles." This is not to say that there is never any efficacy in trying, but it is to say that in all aspects of doing some things and some aspects of doing all things it is not only unnecessary but detrimental to try. In this matter judo can supplement traditional education.

Implicit but not explicit in Huxley's article is a related matter that deserves comment. A judo student must learn not only to let himself act without much conscious interference, but also to let external events take their own course without forcing their conclusion. This is a subtler meaning of the instruction to let the adversary throw himself.

Letting events follow their own course is important in sport judo, but in serious fighting it is vital, because of its effect on both fighting efficiency and moral consequences. For as the full consummation of love is the creation of new life, the full consummation of serious conflict is death. Every fighter inflicts damage, and is, insofar, a killer. Any serious fight may result in death. The only moral way for a man to fight is to let the adversary throw himself—let events follow their own course.

The ancient Zen swordmasters handled themselves and their battles in this way. A swordmaster entered a state of no-mind, simply responding to the situation as it existed in its moment in time and point in space, letting his own "not-self" function as well as the self and non-self of the adversary and *of the process itself.* If either he or the adversary pushed the fight to its conclusion and died, so it had to be. It must be remembered that the swordmaster, like the Judoka, was a difficult man to get into a fight. He would avoid it until an adversary or a situation forced one on him. The adversary who forces a fight on such a man (even if he does not know that the man is a swordmaster) is in a way committing suicide. Killing under these circumstances is neither more nor less moral than making love under circumstances that call for making love. But *any* forcing, *any at all*, is ultimate immorality. The swordmaster had to be certain of his ground—of his attitude—when he killed. Otherwise, he inevitably found himself in a hell of his own making.

The swordmaster's rule seems to me a good one for judomen. A judoman has a slight advantage, too, over the swordmaster in that it is easier to show mercy in unarmed combat than in swordplay.

Emphasis on not trying and on letting be should not be taken as suggesting absolute lack of value in traditional discipline and even in "trying hard." Blake's dictum still holds: whatever can be believed is an image, however distorted, of the truth. The Judoka does have his students practice "techniques" (standard throwing maneuvers) and attempt the standard forms of the throws.

Poetry and judo are analogous regarding the relation of form to freedom. The poet learns a traditional form—say, that of the sonnet—in order to supplement his own content with the strength implicit in that vehicle. He learns to write a sonnet so that he is free to use the sonnet form when the effect he desires to create calls for that form. So the judo student learns the "technique." Techniques are not rules or enslaving devices to limit the freedom of the judoman. They are simply methods, prepared in advance of the occasion and to be modified as the occasion demands, of taking advantage of kuzushi. The judoman disciplines himself (i.e. makes his movements conform to the standard) in practice in order to be free to use the techniques when opportunity arises. Freedom grows out of discipline. Spontaneity is not incompatible with practice. Indeed, the converse is true.

But standard form is not to be taken as an absolute. The standard form as a mere complex of movements would be difficult to learn for a student who tried to impose it on an incompatible life style, and such a student would be utterly incapable of maintaining any spontaneity and flow within the form. But, given that compatibility, the standard form can enhance strength and freedom—up to a point. To go still further, the particular judoman must adapt the standard form to his *personal* style. This is why the Judoka encourages Leeda to modify the classical forms in whatever way feels right to her—but *after* she has achieved some degree of mastery of them in their original state.

The only absolute is the relation of form to life style. Thus, the central feature of the Judoka's instruction is the ju-no-kata, the demonstration of ju, which attempts to instill in the student the feel or sense of yielding, poetic movement, love.

The Judoka teaches the young woman as he visited with the boy: getting as well as giving. The Judoka realizes that the best teaching—and the best healing—is a process of exchange, similar to that dramatized in Leeda's dance, in which both give and both take. But in the case of the Judoka and the boy, a healthy adult and a sickly child, what has the child to exchange?

In order to find out, let's carry the boy back a step in imagination and suppose that he is an infant and that he and the Judoka are out on the beach. The Judoka sees a sheet of blue and knows that it is the sky, a sheet of blue-green-gray and knows that it is the ocean, a sheet of light tan and knows that it is the sand. He hears noises and recognizes the lapping of the waves and the call of the gulls. He feels a light pressure on his face and another on his feet realizes that he is standing in the wind on the beach. He sniffs and knows that he is smelling salt air and decaying fish. He touches his hand to his mouth and knows that he is tasting saltwater: The Judoka, being an adult, categorizes these things automatically and files them away in his mind, so to speak; if he is going to pay special attention to one sensation he must do it deliberately and at the cost of ignoring the others. He cannot avoid this categorizing. The infant experiences all of the same sensations, but he does not categorize: for him the sight and sound and feel and smell and taste are one large undifferentiated and unique experience. His experience is more *mythic*, more *poetic*, than the Judoka's. Granted, we want the infant to mature, which means to come to experience as the Judoka does. But we should understand that when he does mature he loses something, and the loss is very real. What he loses is that poetry, that mythic quality, which makes us nostalgic when we smell or see something that reminds us of early childhood. The boy has an exchange for the Judoka in that he is closer to infancy, and thus to poetry, than the Judoka. Every word he says conveys that poetry to an attentive listener, even though much of what he says is silly and hardly any of it gives new information.

The Judoka realizes this and is an attentive listener for the sake of experiencing vicariously that poetry.

The Judoka's exchange with Leeda is more obviously equal. In her dance interpretation of the poem she carries herself and her audience of one to exactly the same point (i.e. makes them arrive at the same attitude) the Judoka is trying to attain for himself and his student by practice of the ju-no-kata. In a way, the exchange is perfectly even; there is no teacher and no student. Yet insofar as judo is concerned the Judoka remains the teacher and Leeda the student, for while Leeda can adopt in her dance the precise attitude that is the key to judo effectiveness, she cannot make the transfer of that attitude in dance to the fighting situation. That is to say, when she moves from an activity in which she is practiced to one in which she is not practiced she loses confidence and the ability to act naturally and freely. She does, then, just what most of us do when we take up a new enterprise—and so we need teachers to help us make the transfer. In theory, and for some people under some circumstances in practice, the transfer is easy to make and no teacher of a specific art is necessary.

Leeda's dance illustrates more vividly than the ju-no-kata one vital aspect of the attitude essential to good judo. In this book I have said a good bit about love of the enemy (or in Jesus's phrase, love of one's neighbor), but I have not said much about Jesus's other instruction—to love the Lord thy God. Leda's encounter with the swan exemplifies the necessary relation of the judoman to the whole, the process behind the whole, the divine, or whatever it is to be called.

Everyone is raped by the gods (I hope that is the case—it is unthinkable that anyone should be left out, should never feel the terrible and joyous thrust of that which seems utterly real) but not everyone responds as Leda does and accepts and appreciates and loves that thrust. The judoman must do so. To put the matter another way, the judoman must love the whole of the human condition in order to accept it and pay close and sympathetic attention to it. Only by so doing does he gain the aliveness that produces a "sixth sense" protecting him so that he need not excessively fear even grouped opponents.

Love, even of the divine, is not altogether happy, as Leeda shows at the conclusion of her dance. For one thing, there are times and ways in which softness is cruelty and love is harsh. For another, beauty and truth perhaps have, but love certainly has, an ephemeral quality in which a sense of loss must always haunt the magic. Soon after Leda's terror of the great bird has passed into a love of him, the swan-god drops her and is gone. She knows then that vast hollowness in the stomach that is the emotion of utter loss. Her ecstasy passes immediately into a despair. So even here, even in the love of God, there is no point gained, no winning. Yet one does not lose either, for the whole experience of pleasure and pain has great value; and perhaps in the very knowledge of it, the very participation in it, one achieves a kind of victory.

The indifference of the girl in the dance is a natural counter to her suffering, and she accepts it exactly as the Judoka accepts fear and anger. By letting her indifference grow and have full play she enables herself to see the other side of her suffering—that despite her loss, she knows now the possibility of the full richness of love.

Readers who regard themselves as post-Christian may be bothered a little by my repeated references to Jesus and my use of phrases like "Love thy God." Readers who regard themselves as orthodox Christian (especially those who are in the puritan tradition) may be upset by my illustration of the love of god by means of a naked woman dancing on a beach for a man to whom she is not married; they may feel that I am being entirely too free in my interpretation of the concepts of love of god and neighbor. The possibility of both kinds of objection demonstrates two of the major problems of teaching: first, that in an important respect any teacher is limited to teaching any student what that student is ripe for or at least willing to learn; and second, that whatever words one chooses may be misleading.

The culture out of which ours grew was Christian, whether our current one is or not, and most of our values emerge from at least a semi-Christian base. Whether for this reason alone or for some other, Jesus exemplifies many of our highest values. I keep mentioning him because I keep seeing ways in which his words or his life illustrate what I am trying to say. As for the matter of the existence of God, we have stumbled around too long questioning the factual status of what strikes me as an essentially poetic concept; it is time for us to move on. And concerning the objection from the opposite camp, let me admit that I may be using the expression "Love thy God" to mean something quite different from what Jesus meant by it. I don't know. All I know is that I am using it to express something that seems meaningful to me.

Leeda's nakedness relates to this objection but has a more far-reaching importance of its own. While we do see her in this scene as an artist, and her nudity can be accounted for in those terms alone and certainly without apology, it is obvious—as she herself recognizes—that she is taking a step in the direction of what people used to call "illicit" love. Our contemporary sexual mores are such that I could easily pass over this matter without comment, but I would like to mention it in order to approach some points that seem to me significant.

The first of these is not original to me. I need it to make sense out of the second one. The romance in which this man and woman are engaged is not, and will not be even if it reaches consummation, either improper or unlawful. The couple is moving stage by stage slowly—perhaps too slowly, for I want to make the point clearly—toward a spiritual union so powerful as to make physical union happen almost of itself. This kind of union is the most proper and lawful of relations between man and woman, regardless of any matters of legal contract. (In fact, I would go so far as to say that marriage exists in a meaningful sense only when this magic is present, matters of legal contract, religious ritual, and temporal permanence notwithstanding *either way*. Physical union in the absence of this magic is wrong, I suspect, again regardless of promises and expectations.) Again I can find support for my view in the words of Jesus, who pointed out the priority of spirit over letter in matters of law.

The second argument, and one I have not seen stated, has to do with the nudity *not* being taken by either the man or the woman as necessarily leading to immediate sexual congress. Conventions in various segments of society establish what degrees of physical intimacy are taken as key positions such that, once they are attained, affairs move automatically to consummation; thus, when the man touches the woman's bare breasts or buttocks, or in some social groups when he kisses her, the preliminaries are over and there is a rush toward hoped-for mutual orgasm. The trouble with this tradition is that it makes several stages of physical intimacy—which should be paralleled by increasing degrees of emotional and mental closeness—either completely unattainable or likely to be passed over too quickly to be appreciated. When this happens, not only is a great deal of pleasure lost, but there is also, inevitably, a measure of illicit love (according to my definition) in the consummation.

In this matter the behavior of the Judoka and Leeda parallels the Judoka's conduct in his fight—there is never any attempt to rest in the automatic; rather, being a participant means to continue to participate. Their behavior also parallels the Judokas method of teaching. He stands at the opposite pole from those who set up systems of curricula geared to an abstraction called "the mass mind."

道
場

It is very early dawn when the Judoka awakens. At this time of day a man who has slept well knows something akin to newness of life, to primeval innocence. Standing, the Judoka, whose tanned body exhibits the strength and fluidity of his manner of living, seems a type of Adam effortlessly exerting his authority over a domain of glistening green bushes, sand, and sea. New life is stirring more vigorously than usual this morning, either in the man himself or in the environment or in both.

The Judoka is in a thoughtful mood this morning, and in a few minutes he puts on a pair of bathing trunks and begins to make coffee. While the water is boiling he gathers some blackberries for a light breakfast. He eats and then, rising on one knee and sipping coffee, he gazes out toward the sea.

He is still in that posture when Leeda arrives. She is again wearing the green bathing suit. When she sees the Judoka she says nothing but goes over to him and stands by his side; her cool thigh touches his arm, and he feels both a desire for her and a present closeness to her exceeding anything he has known. He puts an arm around her hip and holds her, and for the moment that is sufficient.

Later she eats some blackberries and pours herself a cup of coffee. "Maybe I'm flattering myself," she says, "but I get an impression that you are thinking about what happened last night."

"Hmmm," he answers, "I wonder to what degree thought is transferred by touch or just presence? . . . Yes. I was reliving the experience, and then, in a different and perhaps rather curious sort of way I began to think about it."

"What do you mean?"

"With your interpretive dance and your poetry you can do a very interesting sort of thing. You can create atmosphere—psychological atmosphere. And atmosphere is what controls people."

"But I don't want to control anyone," Leeda protests, her brows contracting into a frown.

The Judoka stands and stretches, then kneels and begins repairing the kerosene fire rig. "Don't blame you. Neither does anybody else who has any wisdom—it's a terrible responsibility. But look here: There is always some kind of atmosphere, and in our present state of civilization people make the most of it. But the greater part of that which gets made is made carelessly and unknowingly and badly. Certain kinds of atmosphere—that you made last night, or that you and I made together this morning—free people; other kinds enslave them. The people who make the atmosphere are the rulers—atmosphere is the principal device of rule, incidentally, as well as the chief product of it.

The woman brushes her hair out of her face. "However that may be, I myself don't want to rule anything," she says.

"Neither do I," he agrees, "and I don't often like to fight either, but sometimes it's necessary to fight and sometimes it's necessary to rule."

She puckers her mouth, hesitates, and then asks, "How does atmosphere rule?"

"By determining attitude," he says, taking more coffee. "Or going a long way toward doing so."

Leeda shifts again into a sitting position, but she makes no comment.

"Imagine how well I could teach judo if I could establish an atmosphere in which a person almost *had* to have the correct attitude, couldn't avoid it. Do you see?" The Judoka shifts his posture, going up on to one knee. "Have you ever seen a judo show?"

The woman's eyes brighten. "No," she says, "but I'd like to."

"Most of them are pretty amateurish. The idea is to show people what the art or sport is. A group of kids in gis haul out a mat and do a series of forward rolls slapping the mat and yelling kiai! to sound bloody. Then somebody, usually the instructor, goes to a microphone and tells a little about the history of judo, Kano and all that, and then the group gives demonstration throws. Often it winds up with a comedy routine of a girl turning the tables on a thug who is attacking her . . . It goes over great with high school audiences."

"Nobody breaks any boards?"

"Sometimes, but we usually leave that for the karate people. But here's my point: I've been wanting to do a real judo show—one that will describe the Way as it really is and maybe help create the atmosphere I want too, an atmosphere that the people who get interested in can remember and carry with them." The Judoka completes his repair job and sits down. "It seems to me that it would be possible, using the techniques of interpretive dance with some Zen stories and some of the formal katas, to produce such a show."

Leeda sits up alertly as the project begins to take hold of her imagination. "Yes," she says, "aren't there stories about Samurai warriors that would apply? And there's a passage from Huxley . . ."

"There is a story about a teamaster that might begin the show about as well as anything," the Judoka says, "and a letter from a swordmaster named Takuan that would be good."

"How about Lao-tzu?" Leeda asks. "Much of judo seems to follow him."

A long conversation ensues as they mull over ideas for stories and dramatizations and discuss place, time, lighting and publicity. The Judoka's face is that of a business executive figuring out what can be done and how best to do it. Leeda's face is that of an actress planning a show.

"I'd like to use the boy in the show," the man says. "In most of these shows they have a girl being attacked and repelling her attacker. Maybe we could have a little kid being kidnapped by a woman and getting away?"

The woman laughs. "You can't do that," she says. "You can't have some boy beating up on a woman, even if she is kidnapping him. It's contrary to the whole American way of life! We'd be run out of town." The more she thinks of it, the funnier it gets.

"Well—" says the Judoka, grinning at his own idea. "Let me put up this coffee rig, and we'll get started.

"Maybe we can use the boy to do the ju-no-kata with you," he adds.


For the next ten days the Judoka, Leeda, and the boy are fully occupied with the preparations. Leeda, who has considerable experience with dance concerts, lends technical direction related to the actual performance, while the Judoka and the boy, with some aid from the latter's mother, take care of the business matters. The Judoka makes arrangements with the hotel for use of a small outdoor amphitheater dug into an L created by the front of the building and one of its wings. The boy and his mother make notices, and the boy carries them around and places them.

The Judoka thoroughly enjoys playing lightly at being man of affairs but drives his performers unmercifully to mastery of the necessary judo maneuvers. Leeda is mildly amused at the Judoka's enthusiasm and at the absurdity of the company and its make-up, but she herself grows increasingly enthusiastic about the content of the show. The boy remains in a state of rather high excitement despite the Judoka's and Leeda's continued efforts to calm him, yet he looks better, his mother says, than he has in months.

Leeda spends much time on the lighting system. She gets help from the Judoka but little advice—she is managing this phase of the project, he says, and if she is to do it well she must operate so as to express her own personality, thinking, and feeling. This attitude bothers Leeda a little, for she is not fully confident of her ability to handle this aspect of the show. The boy, on the other hand, is delighted to be allowed, for once, to work without a great deal of supervision. Despite the difference in these reactions, both jobs are done well, and so are those that the Judoka does himself. The completed project bears the marks of all three performers, yet the completed project is a harmonious whole.

On the night of the performance about sixty people, hotel guests and townspeople, gather in the amphitheater in the dusk. Fireflies flicker here and there, and a land breeze stirs, carrying the scent of pine. There's a feeling about the occasion similar to that of summer twilight band concerts in small-town parks.

All three performers are on stage and in gis, but the spotlight rests on Leeda alone in the center. The Judoka starts the show by describing an old Japanese teamaster, a man who devoted his life to the ceremonial rite of making and serving tea in a simple hut, thereby providing his guests with a few moments of a unique kind of tranquillity. Leeda acts out the arranging of utensils, the putting of the kettle on the fire, the passing of bowl to guest. She manages to suggest the presence of a bamboo grove, a garden of arranged streams and rocks and bushes. More important, she manages to portray a man who is following a Way in his handling of tea and water and all the details of management of his hut, a man at peace with himself and the world about him, a man sensitive to every nuance of tea and water and kettle and guest . . .

The Judoka relates how one day the old man of peace was set upon and challenged to a duel by sword by an outlaw Samurai warrior. Even to offer such a challenge was unthinkable, and many warriors offered to champion the old teamaster, but he refused. The duel was fought, and to the amazement of all the onlookers, the teamaster killed the outlaw.

Leeda acts out the challenge and the teamaster's haughty but sad acceptance of it. Then in free dance she portrays a moment of despair, a sinking to utter resignation, and a rising to suicidal resolution. She begins to pantomime a fight with a two-handed sword . . .

Continuing, the Judoka tells how the teamaster was questioned about his victory over the experienced fighting man. The teamaster replied that he did not know how he had done it, but that he had practiced the Way in his making of tea and that he had learned how to die.

Leeda's movement with sword and feet are smooth and flowing, but it is her face which is impressive. She conveys an impression of total egolessness. She is an old man open to everything around him, an old man with awakened senses, alert and responsive and spontaneous, an old man who actually loves the enemy who is trying to kill him with hard steel. Members of the audience, who have come casually to see a crude demonstration on the beach, find themselves shocked and breathless. The Judoka himself is speechless for a moment, for the girl is going far beyond what she has ever achieved in rehearsal.

As the aged victor is refreshed and supported by a small boy— and the audience bursts forth with spontaneous applause—the Judoka comments. To learn to die, it is of course necessary to learn to live. The man shown making tea revealed that he had learned to live in the manner in which he made the tea. Any art that is part of a Way is at once living and training for that Way. Is it so surprising, then, that a person who has mastered the Way in one of its art forms should be able to shift to another art and funnel the Way through this new channel? Judo, the speaker continues, is simply another art form for the expression of the teamaster's Way, and it has fully as much value for the making of tea as it does for defending oneself in the street.

There is a pause, and then the Judoka describes the discovery of the principle of ju-jitsu by a Buddhist monk who observed that the oak limb breaks under the weight of snow while the willow yields to the snow, drops it off, and returns in freedom to its place, Leeda translates the words into dance and then leaves the spotlight.

The boy moves into the spotlight while Leeda narrates the history of judo, telling about the slow decay and death of ju-jitsu and of the regret of the boy and young man, Jigaro Kano, who enjoyed the martial arts and thought he saw in them much of value for human development. The Judoka steps into the spotlight, and the boy, now playing the small and aged founder of judo—a refined and safer-to-practice version of ju-jitsu—throws the man three times, one of them with the beautiful *tomoe-nage*, or wheel throw, which draws from the audience another spontaneous ovation.

Leeda's voice fades and is replaced by the Judoka's. In the background now come soft strains of minor-key Oriental music. The Judoka returns to the matter of the teamaster's willingness to die and relates it to a conception of self and existence that permits a person to live in the moment, so to love and meet whatever comes in the moment in the state of no-mind.

The Judoka reads part of Suzuki's translation of a letter by the ancient Zen swordmaster Takuan, who says that the wisdom called no-mind is intuitively acquired after a great deal of practical training. Leeda is performing a gymnastic dance, moving from one yoga posture to another in a delightful training pattern. The Judoka continues, quoting Takuan's assertion that the wisdom called no-mind holds a high degree of motility with a center that remains immobile. When this state is attained, he says, the mind reaches a high point of alacrity, ready to direct its attention anywhere it is needed.

The boy's voice now replaces the Judoka's. Leeda and the Judoka enter the circle of light and engage in a light randori, a trading of throws, with the grace and ease appropriate to a ballroom. The boy explains that Takuan's instructions are to a swords-man, but in substance and as they apply to an unarmed fighter they are that he should not let his attention be engaged and arrested by the hands and feet of the adversary, for when he does this he loses the opportunity to make the next move by himself— he tarries and thinks, and while this deliberation is going on, the adversary catches him off balance. The fighter should not present this opportunity. He must follow the hands of the adversary but leave his mind free to make its own countermovements without his interfering deliberation. He must move as the opponent moves.

Takuan asserts that this non-interfering attitude constitutes the most vital element in the fighter's art. If there is any room left between two actions "even for the breadth of a hair," he says, this room is interruption. If the fighter is troubled and deliberate about what to do in anticipation of an adversary's attack, he leaves room—that is, a good opportunity for attack. The proper way for the fighter to act is illustrated by what happens when a man claps his hands: the sound issues forth without a moment's deliberation; it does not stop and think before it issues. There is no mediacy: one action follows another without interruption by the conscious mind. Takuan advises the fighter to let the defense follow the attack without an instant's cogitation so that *there will be no two separate movements of attack and defense.*

The Judoka and the girl perform the push-pull exercise with hands and feet and with all actions exaggerated. The music stops.

Finally, the boy says, Takuan advises that if all this is understood in terms of quickness, the understanding is incorrect. The idea is immediateness of action, an uninterrupted flow of life energy. The fighter should cultivate this flow.

It is now quite dark, save for a few fireflies, the stars, and the circle of light. The Judoka stands in the circle alone. Leeda speaks, cautioning her listeners that all this is not to suggest that there is no quickness in judo or no violence. Judo at its climax is like a high wind . . . Suddenly the Judoka turns, screams Kiai! and dives and slaps. He stands again, a savage figure, and lashes out with his feet at an imagined opponent. The audience, lulled by the grace and quiet flow of the previous action, is shocked and stirred.

Leeda continues, pointing out that the importance of no-mind is that it permits love; permits one to let everything in the world, including one's enemy, be what it wills to be. (One does not love a person when one wants to change him—one loves the idealized conception into which one is trying to make him.) Leeda narrates, and the Judoka portrays, the story of Morihei Uyeshiba in a cottage yard, pouring water over his body and looking up into the blue sky. Uyeshiba had studied the martial arts for years and loved them but had come to doubt their value—what good is victory save to satisfy vanity, which is of no value? On this occasion, the earth suddenly trembled, and Uyeshiba saw a golden vapor gushing out of the earth enveloping his body, and then he felt himself tumbling into a golden body. He understood what the birds were saying, he surrendered his own small ego and made the spirit of nature his own mind. And in that instant he understood that the fundamental principle of the martial arts is universal love. He later founded the Way called aikido, in some respects an advanced form of judo, which aims not so much at victory as at maintaining the flow of life through all creatures.

The voice now changes, as the boy speaks, saying that others have anticipated Uyeshiba in this matter. He quotes Lao-tzu on compassion, the one wealth that can afford the enemy, and Jesus on loving the enemy and turning the other cheek. Leeda demonstrates how turning the other cheek is a form of the yielding way. Now comes the voice of the Judoka: "But let's not oversimplify or try to convert what is sometimes hard into something that is always soft. The teamaster loved his enemy, but he killed him. Takuan is one of the swordmasters who suggest that the true master never really kills his adversary, but that sometimes he must let the adversary kill himself. Love has several faces, and some of them are hard and apparently cruel. Strife is the converse side of love and is as necessary to love as night is to day. Heraclitus asserts that Homer was wrong in wishing that strife might perish from among gods and men. Homer did not see, Heraclitus says, that he was praying for the destruction of the universe; for, if his prayer were heard, all things would pass away."

The Judoka's tone changes and he describes the ju-no-kata, saying that it is a ceremonial training sequence designed to impress upon the minds and bodies of the participants the principle of ju, that face of love or yielding or gentleness or the poetic which is the heart of ju-do, the Way of Ju. Upon the completion of this exercise, the Judoka announces, he and his companions will conclude the show with a series of kata—formal exhibitions of sequences of throws.

The woman and the boy bow to each other in the spotlight and go through the stylized forms of the ju-no-kata. They are nearly finished when the show is violently interrupted.

Five motorcycles roar over the top of the mound that forms the edge of the amphitheater; they wheel in dangerously close to the last row of chairs, brake, and gun their engines. The dress and manner of the riders indicate that they are a local group of would-be Hell's Angels. The leader, a huge young man with the name "Tiny" painted across his leather jacket, addresses the crowd: "What's going on here? This guy in the white pajamas showing you how to fight? Wonder if he really knows how?"

Like the audience, Leeda and the boy are shocked. The Judoka is surprised but not upset. He is elated. He feels no fear at all, although at times when he has seen similar things happen in films he has thought them frightening. There flickers through his mind a recognition that he is not afraid, and that he has consequently lost a powerful ally; but there is nothing to be done about it—there is no time to create fear even though he may need it. Elation crowds out any concern. What more beautiful way of ending a judo show could he have devised? He has a momentary doubt: will the audience think it arranged? What irony!

The audience, however, has no such notion. There is a murmuring, and people are standing and gathering up children. One can feel in the air an anticipation of panic or rout. Thus is atmosphere created, Leeda thinks, and thus does it rule; and she hates herself for thinking it.

But now the Judoka steps into the circle of light. His very walk is regal, for he recognizes that he has command of this situation in a more profound sense than anyone else there can suppose. "Keep your places," he says, not loudly but in a more authoritative tone than Leeda has ever heard him use. Everyone obeys instantly and without question; even the feet of the cyclists freeze momentarily on their accelerators. Leeda is strangely detached from the event. To her own surprise, she finds herself contrasting the Judoka's manner now with that he used in asking her to dance: she reflects that there is a difference in the command that is pleasant, inevitable, and foregone, and the one that is painful but necessary to the deflecting of danger.

Tiny regains his poise. "Come on down, man, and show us how you do it," he taunts.

The Judoka is an inexperienced actor, and before he can stop himself, he smiles. "All right," he says. But he recovers and makes his face a mask as he steps forward to the edge of the earthen stage. He pauses to address his audience: "I apologize for this, although certainly I am not responsible for it. Nevertheless, it's not altogether bad. You came to see an exhibition of judo. You are about to see one." He turns to the stage. "Leeda," he says, "if you can, please keep the light on me." He turns back to the audience. "The highest form of judo is simply to turn aside the hostility of the adversary, to control his spirit, and perhaps to turn him away. If I can do that, I will—"

"Yeah, I bet ya'd like that," yells one of the riders, laughing.

"If, however, I can't," the Judoka continues, "I ask you to remember that I have already said that the love that gives root to true judo has hardness as well as softness." He pauses again, and he is an awesome figure as he stands relaxed but ready at the edge of the light.

Four of the cyclists look to Tiny, a bit nervously now.

"One more thing—"

"Come on, quit stalling."

The Judoka looks at the cyclist and, this time, grins. The absurdity of the yell becomes apparent. "—since this act will conclude our show, whatever happens," he continues. "I remember a story John Thomason tells about a backwoods Texas circuit-riding preacher. It may be bad art to descend from the level of the formal Asiatic to that of the frontier humor of the American Southwest, but I'm American and so are you people, and since we can never take to ourselves the East in its pure form, we have to translate as best we can into our own ways of seeing and acting; so maybe my story is appropriate as a conclusion. Anyway, this tall, rawboned Texan arrived at his meeting house one Sunday morning to find his way blocked by a couple of tough characters. 'What are ya gonna do, Preacher, if we don't letcha in?' The circuit rider thought for a minute, and then he said, 'Well, boys, I'll tell you: If the Holy Spirit grant me the grace, I'll turn aside. But if He don't, Lord have mercy on your souls!' . . . That's about our situation here."

Suddenly but easily, walking with no hesitation at all, the Judoka starts up the aisle. Leeda keeps the spotlight on him.

"Hey, guys, what if the cops come?" asks one of the cyclists.

That is enough excuse for the two boys in the rear. They gun and dig out and are off. The third follows in near panic. Tiny and his number two look at each other as the Judoka approaches, and Tiny decides to put the best possible face on the matter: "Oh you've frightened us away," he yells in his highest falsetto, and he and his friend are gone. The act is not convincing.

The Judoka turns and walks back to the stage as the admiring crowd begins to break up.

道
場

Making, when that which is being made is too large or too complex for one man to handle, or when that which is being made is community itself, requires men to extend themselves and merge their extensions to form a new animal, collective or corporate man. In corporate as in individual man the head serves a necessary function. Ruling is but one aspect of making, but it is a highly important one.

For the moment I am not concerned with the question of whether the function of head should be exercised by one man or jointly by all of the people who comprise the corporate animal. What I have to say applies to both conditions. My concern here is with the qualities and attitudes of a person that permit him to rule well, whether he has but a one-vote share in the ruling or does the whole job. The Judoka is twice cast in the role of executive, once because he finds or conceives a project that seems worthwhile, and once because he finds himself in an emergency with which no one else is prepared to cope.

We have several names for the executive, and since it seems very likely that the words we choose influence our thinking and consequent behavior, our selection of the proper one is a crucial matter. We can call him a foreman or a chairman or an administrator or a director or a manager or a governor or a president or a king, just to mention a few of the possibilities. (That we have usually reserved the word *king* for the head of a state is to me only a historical oddity, for it seems to me that ruling a state is precisely paralleled by ruling a business or a university or a club.) The polar opposites are *manager* and king. The word *manager* connotes a dry, almost faceless entity immersed in ledger sheets and lost in abstractions. The word *king* carries with it pageantry and splendor. It produces images of a strong man, a man at once earthy and godlike. I think we shall not have anything like an ideal society until our managers give way before kings.

There have been bad or weak kings, of course, but these do not deserve the term as I am using it here. I am using it in its ideal sense, and I am interested in the regal quality in any man that permits him to rule himself as well as others. The judoman must either have this quality or develop it, even if he never rules anyone but himself or, at most, himself and his adversary. He must have it because it is both the cause and effect of the attitude essential to good judo. Since judo both requires and develops the quality, the judoman is inescapably a ruler.

In governing himself, a man naturally gives as much regard to his hands and feet and other parts as to his head. The Judoka's regard is not only a concern for the welfare of these parts of his body; it is also a respect for them and a willingness to give them the freedom to act as seems best to them, yet under his direction. Just as the Judoka and his adversary and the pattern of the developing throw jointly determine the outcome of the throw, so the Judoka's head and the rest of his person jointly determine his own part in the event. (I realize the absurdity of talking about the Judoka as if he were his head to some greater degree than he is some other part. This, however, is the common conception, and it is useful here in making clear the relation between the "whole Judoka" and his several parts. Another way to put this would be to say that the Judoka thinks with his hands and his feet as well as his intellect.)

In governing the corporate person, the true king remembers that this intangible "man" is an extension of himself. He has the same concern for the "least" of his subjects as he does for himself. He has respect for his subjects and a willingness to yield to them a great deal of freedom in determining how they shall act.

What this amounts to is that the true king or manager so designs and maintains his organization that each member of it can be a maker in the full sense of that word: i.e. can express—press out from—himself in some product, tangible or intangible, that will bear the marks of his own personality and thereby be satisfying to him and fulfilling of him. To be a true maker, a person must be whole; it is the principal task of management or government to set conditions under which each member of the organization or the state is encouraged and enabled to live in such a way that he can do just that. Abraham Maslow calls the kind of administration that functions in this way "eupsychian management." In the final analysis, it is the only genuinely intelligent kind of management.

When the king governs in this way, the large or complex product of the organization—whether it be a manufactured item or society itself—can be constructed in the same spirit of love in which the individual craftsman gives birth to his creations. This kind of product is the only one worthwhile.

It is obvious that the main purpose of a state is the welfare of its citizens. It should be equally obvious that the main purpose of a business is the welfare of the people who work in it; yet traditionally we have been inclined to lose sight of that purpose in our enthusiasm over productivity or profit. Somewhere recently I read about an old cobbler shop in which was posted a sign to the effect that the primary business of the shop was not the making of shoes but the making of men. The proprietor of that shop was a eupsychian manager, one who realized that his firm existed not only to pay his men a salary but also to enable them to grow and develop as human beings and to live full lives, and one who realized also that under these conditions the making of good shoes would come virtually of itself.

But if this building of men is the prime purpose of organization, and if, as seems likely, a leader cannot fully delegate any of his principal responsibilities, then the statesman must be something more than a political or military strategist and the captain of industry something more than a comptroller or design engineer. The king must be in a very real sense healer and teacher of his people.

In the king everything that we have said or will say about the Judoka comes together. The king must be a fighter, usually to become king and probably always to maintain his kingdom. He must be a lover in order to be a fighter and certainly in order to govern in accordance with the principles we are laying down. He must be a hunter, at least in the broad sense in which we have used the term, and he must hunt diligently for wisdom if he is to approach the stature of Plato's philosopher-king. We have already asserted that he must be healer and teacher, for his whole job is the building of men. He must be a maker, either of the state or of something else too large or too complex for a single individual to handle.

But, most important, he must be a maker of mood. As far as I know, no one has done a definitive study of what we call, for lack of a better word, atmosphere, but the matter is well worth study, for I suspect that a very great deal depends on atmosphere. I can't define what I'm discussing, but I can give examples of it: The French Quarter in New Orleans has a distinctive flavor or mood that one senses as soon as one steps into it and that somehow governs almost everything done in that section of the city; the Garden District of the same city, out along St. Charles Avenue, has an entirely different flavor or mood that works in the same way. The campus of every major university that I know anything about has a kind of special climate, an electricity in the air that one can feel and that we usually describe as "intellectually stimulating."

I cannot prove anything about atmosphere; all I can do is assert. And I assert unhesitatingly that campus atmosphere has more to do with education—affects it more, either positively or negatively—than classroom buildings or libraries or even faculties. And I suspect that the atmosphere of a business affects the quality of the work done there, and that of a state the quality of the living done there, just as the atmosphere of a restaurant affects the quality of the eating done there.

The Judoka suggests that the making of mood is the chief method by which the king rules. The king does not make that mood by himself, however, nor does he even determine by himself what that mood is going to be. If he does his job correctly, he makes atmosphere as the Judoka makes a fishnet, letting the cord find its own lay, but expressing his own personality in the product. The king must set conditions under which the natural and unique mood of his people may develop, yet he must ensure that the mood develops as a poetic one. The king, then, is a maker of poetic mood or atmosphere—which is to say that the king is a poet. I do not mean that he writes necessarily (although I think it interesting that Churchill and De Gaulle and Kennedy were writers) but that he makes what may be called "field poetry"—poetry written in the wind, in the affairs of state.

Genuine poetry is produced only as the honest expression of a person whose life is in some way poetic. The king rules best, therefore, as the teacher teaches best or the healer heals best, not so much by anything he does as by what he is; by simply being. The best king, then, is the whole man, the one who is fully and poetically alive.

It is apparent that the true king will not lose his regal quality when he loses his crown. It should be equally apparent that the growth of that quality does not depend on the holding of a position of authority. It is a quality that every man may have and should have—for it is as essential in ruling oneself as in ruling a nation. Huey Long's old slogan, "Every man a king," has merit.

# 知 KNOWING

A heavy, dark-blue storm cloud makes the early evening dark, and a scent of approaching rain is in the air. Three motorcyclists, Tiny and his number two and three, are cruising along the beach.

"Well, whadayewknow," Tiny says, braking and pointing ahead. "Thar she blows! as the sailors say."

"What?" asks number two.

"Don't you see? That man and woman there. That's her buddy, White Pajamas. Only he's in a bathing suit this time."

Lightning streaks the air, and in the flash the couple is clearly identifiable. From his saddlebag the number two man extracts a length of chain. "Let's go after 'em," he says.

Number three arms himself with a short section of hard rubber hose. Tiny, flexing his massive muscles, has no need of weapons. He revs his engine. "Let's go!" he commands.

The three cyclists draw up in a line confronting the Judoka and the young woman. The men say nothing, but park their bikes and step forward, Tiny in the center. Number two twirls the chain; number three slaps his hose against his hand.

The Judoka pays no attention to these signs of nervousness, but to Leeda the slapping of the hose is ominous. There is still no fear in the Judoka, and this time the matter gives him a little concern: once was not too bad, but twice is too much. He is perhaps getting overconfident. Still—he must work with what comes.

Whether or not he is making a mistake that may sometime be costly, for the moment his obvious combination of ease and readiness are disconcerting. His adversaries falter.

But now the Judoka makes what for him is a very unusual kind of mistake. Perhaps he has been too involved lately, too wrapped up in the production of the show, and thus has unwittingly altered his life style sufficiently to interfere with his practice of the Way. Whatever the reason, he permits his mind to wander from the present crisis to the very thing that is making him underrate the crisis—his overconfidence. Vanity perhaps, over the success of the show or his own handling of these very men? Inwardly he smiles, realizing how directly and emphatically the fates often cure the disease of overconfidence; but somehow he does not apply any corrective to his own present circumstance.

His attitude, now lacking the quality that gives him his prime strength, shows in his face. Leeda is watching him, and her faith in him is shaken. Tiny sees him and is no longer intimidated. A few drops of rain fall, the lightning cracks, and Tiny attacks.

Respectful despite himself, Tiny stops short of the Judoka and reaches out for him to pull him within range of his fist. The Judoka merely steps in with the pull, hooks his foot around the inside of Tiny's ankle, and pushes. Tiny falls backward, and the Judoka follows him down, planting a knee in his stomach. Leeda is not on this occasion frozen by the very fact of physical combat. She rushes at the man with the chain, but in the flurry of battle she has forgotten all about no-mind and technique, and with one rough backhand the man knocks her away. The man with the hose rushes in and strikes at the Judoka's head; he misses but strikes the shoulder. Despite the sharp pain, the Judoka grabs the man's wrist with both hands, rises twisting, and using the arm as a lever throws the man over his shoulder.

Just as the Judoka has expected, one man gets in another's way, and the fight is really with one man at a time. But now Leeda is back in the tangle and doing a fairly good job of tying up the man with the hose. The Judoka sees, however, that she is handling herself wildly and leaving herself open to injury, and he makes a double error in judgment to compound his earlier error in attitude: momentarily he diverts his whole attention to her, and he calls to her to back off. In the moment of distraction—his and hers—the woman is thrown roughly to the ground, and Tiny's fist crashes into the side of the Judoka's head. He is dazed. Number two lashes his ankle with the chain and jerks. As the Judoka falls, the man with the hose pounds at his head and shoulders.

Thunder and rain seem to drive the men forward, flailing viciously at the weakened Judoka. The Judoka is about to lose consciousness, and he would like to let go. But deep inside him is the knowledge that yielding to that impulse would be surrender, and he is not quite ready for that. He is now almost insensitive to the blows. He manages to draw back a leg, and then he waits. Finally the moment comes, and the Judoka's foot snaps forward and crashes into Tiny's scrotum. Tiny screams. As the other men pause, the Judoka rouses himself into a sitting posture and an appearance of being again ready to fight. At that moment, Leeda sees someone coming along the beach and screams for help. Tiny's two cohorts hustle their hurt leader aboard his cycle and the three men depart before the assistance arrives.

The Judoka falls back, letting the rain wash over him, as Leeda, jarred but otherwise unhurt, gets to him. Blood is all over his face and neck. As the rain cleans off his body it reveals his shoulders and back and sides seamed with long welts from the hose; it reveals also an ugly chain cut and bruise about the ankle.

Using the only thing available, wet sand, the woman stops the heavy bleeding. She looks up to see what happened to the man to whom she called for help, and she sees him still walking; she starts to yell for him to hurry, and then she recognizes him: it is the redhaired man the Judoka fought on the day she met him. She catches her breath and freezes. Tears well up in her eyes.

The redhead stops, but he simply looks and does nothing. Events and images, like words, gain meaning in part from what one brings to them. The redhead sees this beaten and bleeding man, but the sight conjures up no sympathy. It generates instead a renewal of the humiliation he felt on that other day when he realized that he had led a gang assault on a single man and then lost the battle. It generates too a desire for a rematch. Not now, of course, with the man already beaten, although there must be some compensation for the Judoka's special knowledge. Most important, the sight generates the slight headache the redhead feels just above his eyes whenever he thinks of this man. It is an ache related to humiliation and frustration and some inscrutable thing about this man—some alliance between the man and those intangible forces which so often oppose the redhead—that is chiefly what he hates. He walks on, a white-faced, redhaired man who is alone and bitter as he attempts to cope with an abstraction that to him seems vividly concrete.

Leeda now cries in relief. The rain, gentler now, revives the Judoka. He begins to move around slightly and gently, testing for areas of special pain. He vetoes her suggestion that they try to get to a hospital and asks her to help him out to the water. There he washes ankle and face with saltwater and then spits and gets no blood from inside. "Let's get back to the camp," he says.

Back at the enclosure, reasonably comfortable on his sleeping bag, he asks Leeda if she will stay with him. She laughs. "You couldn't get rid of me," she says.

Then she grows serious. "But I should go get some medicine or a doctor," she says.

"Saltwater is a good medicine," he replies, "and you are all the doctor I need unless we run into complications."

"Anyway, you're a kind of a doctor yourself," the girl says.

"Yes," the Judoka agrees, "but a physician is of not much more use in healing himself than an attorney is in representing himself or a professor in teaching himself." He is quiet for a while, and then he adds: "Don't even let yourself want to cure me . . . You recall the massage I gave the boy? Well, I'd like you to do something like that, very gently, now and then. That's all, besides being here."

"All right," the young woman says, "but not letting myself want to cure is going to be difficult."


Late in the night the Judoka awakens; Leeda, who has been sleeping very lightly beside him, awakens too. The air is rainwashed and fresh, the clouds gone, the stars extraordinarily bright. The woman raises herself on one elbow and looks at the man, but he seems to need nothing.

"There's a mosquito on your stomach," she says. "Are you just going to let him eat, or have you given up enough blood for the day?"

The Judoka chuckles. "Let 'im eat," he says.

She watches until the mosquito flies away, and then she watches the man's stomach. Nothing happens. She feels with her fingers. Nothing. "What is this with you and the mosquitoes?" she asks.

Again he chuckles. "A long time ago I read in a book by a man named R. M. Bucke, a friend of Whitman's, that mosquitoes never seemed to bother Whitman. Then much later I read a comment by Aleister Crowley—you know, the magician'?—that the way to handle mosquitoes is simply to love them. The idea intrigued me. After all, the swelling and the itching are caused by your own body as much as by what the mosquito does. So if you don't resent the mosquito—he has an ecological function to perform, you know, and he doesn't eat much—your body won't react unpleasantly. The whole thing seemed to me to make sense, and Whitman probably loved mosquitoes; he loved everything else, why should mosquitoes be an exception?"

Leeda brushes back her hair and objects: "But this swelling and resenting. You're mixing the physical and the mental."

"Do it all the time," the man replies. "Quite often when I look at you, for example."

The young woman cocks her head and frowns. "That's right," she says. "Some of my professors claim the distinction between mind and body is purely linguistic . . . Maybe it is . . ."

"Sometimes I get to taking the mosquitoes for granted, figuring I've taken care of the problem, you see? Then the itching starts again. There must be something to learn from that." The expression on the Judoka's face is rather wry. "The world has its way of correcting us," he adds. "It certainly took care of my vanity problem today."

Leeda shifts again onto her back, and for a long time the man and woman lie still, saying nothing, looking up at the stars.

"A few years ago, I was lonesome most of the time," the Judoka says slowly. "People around me were busy and sociable and in touch with each other. I was somehow apart, except for an occasional girl or small group, and even then I lost my apartness only for a little while and never quite fully. Conversation hardly ever touched what I was interested in. What people were busy doing seemed to me of no importance at all. Nor did it seem pleasurable. I guess I felt a little the way one of those real judo masters at the Kodokan in Tokyo would feel around a group of just ordinary judo students—that he was hearing a good bit of conversation that didn't mean much and seeing a lot of excess activity that didn't do much. Yet I don't mean that I felt a great deal superior . . . "

The Judoka is quiet for a while. Then he continues: "That parallel is closer than I thought. Because it isn't that the *dan*, the master, knows much—if he feels as I do, that I know hardly anything; it's that he sees how little the others know and how much of their activity doesn't even count. That's the way I felt; but there the parallel stops. I didn't feel I had reached a plateau that was in any way higher. It was lower. The world, for me, wasn't anything; there were just a lot of people who thought it was something. And I envied them: I wished I could think it was something too."

Again the Judoka falls silent. The woman wants to reply, Yes, I've felt that way too; but she decides that would sound too much like making agreeable conversation. She says nothing. She sits up, turns, and begins to make coffee. The Judoka rolls over onto his stomach to watch her. After a while he begins again:

"Then things changed. I seemed to break through into another world. The chaos was gone and I saw a new kind of order and everything was meaningful again. Only now the meaning was on the inside of things, built into them, instead of on the outside. Meaning and being were all the same. I was no longer lonesome. First the stars and the green grass seemed to become parts of me, and then everything did. So I was no longer apart, I was in everything—it was all part of me. Sometimes it was the other way around: there were just stars and green grass and ocean; I wasn't there at all. But since there was no I, I wasn't apart. Everything was me . . . It just went through me . . . Then people began to seem like the stars and the grass. What they did and said was still absurd, but I was them and they were me. I was interested in them and in communication with them and could even share in their business, even though for me it was all a game. It was a delightful and exciting and dramatic game. Even when I felt separate, my separateness was delightful. That's the way it is now."

Handing him a cup of coffee, Leeda smiles and says, "You must be the only person I know who has won the game. Except, maybe me. I'm beginning to get the notion that I may win too."

The Judoka's smile fades, and he shakes his head. "No. I don't want to win, but I haven't anyway. What I have described is the way it is most of the time. But not always. I have occasional periods of what I call 'vastation.' I can't describe them, but they're bleak and barren and nauseous and agonizing. When I'm in that mood I would die, only that seems nauseous too."

He shudders. The young woman moves to his side, puts an arm around his shoulders, and pulls his head to her breast.

"You'd better go to sleep," she says.

"I'm not in that mood now," he says. "But even the remembrance of it—and the knowledge that it will come again—is . . . terrible.

"I know what it is," he continues. "It is the other side of the ecstasy that I know most of the time. It is the horror, just as tangibly a part of the whole as the joy. The joy is inexpressible and is worth the horror. But when I experience the vastation I pay full price for the joy."

He looks at the woman and smiles. "But if you will, Leeda, comfort me anyway," he says. He puts his head down against her bosom and lays a hand across her hip.

知

Irony, that quality of judo which makes it uniquely poetic, lies at the very center of human experience. The world itself is ironic, always going two directions at once—not trying to, but actually doing it, and so maintaining itself in eternal balance. Perhaps the most profound of ironies is the paradox I have identified as the first step of real education: that to go up is to go down, that winning is also losing and losing is also winning, and thus that no one always or in all respects wins—or loses. On this occasion we see the Judoka lose a fight.

His loss is attributable to his own distraction. During his first fight on the beach he made use of his own fear and let it destroy his ego and thereby save him. He wiped his mind clear of self and all else and engaged his adversaries in a no-mind condition, completely caught up in the action of the moment and responding to actual current movements. In that attitude and with his command of technique so well practiced as to be second nature, he had no trouble winning the fight. The number of opponents was not particularly important; as he recognizes, only one or two persons at a time can very well get at a single human target, so the amount of *effective* opposition at any given moment is fairly well limited. (I don't wish to make this sound too easy, but a fighting man with good perception and response can usually handle a multiple-opponent situation much better than a statistical comparison of the number of arms and legs on each side would suggest.) The use of weapons in the second fight was not the significant difference between the two occasions; guns or even knives would have been more important, but the weapons these men used magnified their own prowess only slightly. The whole difference lay in the Judoka's failure in the second fight to abandon himself fully to the moment.

Distracted, the Judoka made two mistakes. The first and less grave of these prevented the Judoka from making a near-perfect response to his problem as at one point he was about to do.

No doubt the perfect response to a conflict situation is Jesus's turning of the other cheek. There are several ways in which this turning of cheek can be done. One is to turn completely around with the blow, almost three hundred and sixty degrees, so that the other cheek comes to the fore. This, of course, is judo. It amounts to a sort of resistance by dodging, and managed perfectly it has the effect of permitting the adversary to frustrate and then throw himself. The Judoka comes close to doing this with the man with the hose. But I suspect that Jesus meant by turning the other cheek simply taking the blow. A person can do this without getting badly hurt. The damage inflicted by a blow has two causes: the force of the blow and the resistance of the object struck. To offer no resistance at all would be to resist by dodging in the manner already mentioned—which is paradoxical. A more complete non-resistance would be to allow the blow to strike. A person willingly permitting a blow to strike his cheek would be unlikely to resist so strongly as to suffer great injury: he would naturally give with the punch. His action would have the advantage of not frustrating the adversary and of letting the adversary express himself in precisely the fashion he has in mind—thus letting him work off his aggressive urge. This response, then, would be one of love in its highest expression.

There is a possibility that a person taking the attitude Jesus suggests would not be attacked at all. Jay Haley, in "The Power Tactics of Jesus Christ," maintains that Jesus's advice amounts to a surrender tactic similar to that used by wolves: "When two wolves are in a fight and one is about to be killed," Haley writes, "the defeated wolf will suddenly lift his head and bare his throat to his opponent. The opponent becomes incapacitated and he cannot kill him as long as he is faced with this tactic." This is one possibility; it seems to me that there is another also. It might be that the love expressed by a turn-the-other-cheek attitude would be contagious and transform the conflict directly into a pure act of love. (Love is contagious. All you have to do to make any person love you is to love him. Our experience sometimes seems to contradict this contention, but only because we very often confuse love with lust or with sentimentality or with a desire for convenience.) But either way, a person could not take such an attitude in the expectation or hope that it would so work out: to do that would be to transform the love into mere weakness and would have the opposite effect; the willingness to be struck and thereby to assist the adversary must be there.

This willingness to be struck in order to help is almost a definition of love, and considering it can serve to demonstrate the effectiveness of love of the enemy. Imagine yourself attacked by someone so important to you that his welfare—which would include at this time his getting "out of his system" (expressing) whatever is bothering him—is of more concern to you than your own. When he strikes you, you are happy that he is striking; you don't want to interfere with his working through his trouble, so you are pleased that his hands and feet go wherever they wish. (The correct attitude here could easily degenerate into, but is absolutely distinct from, a sloppy sentimentality; the two attitudes differ as strength differs from weakness.) Do you see that, although you may be banged up a little, you are in complete command of this kind of situation—that there is no way in which your adversary can force a break between your will and what happens? Your adversary becomes like a small child you are humoring. Further, do you see that the fight is unlikely to last long, especially if it is true that love begets love? The person who is really able, then, to love his enemy and turn the other cheek can eliminate strife. He resembles the perfect aikidoman described by Tohei who simply guides the spirit of his adversaries, or like the woman I read about a few years ago who can sit down in perfect safety beside strange tigers and panthers. The Judoka always attempts to meet a conflict situation in this way. At the show he succeeded, and later, on the beach he almost succeeded again. It was because he demonstrated this attitude that his adversaries faltered. But the Judoka was not on this occasion perfect, and he faltered too.

Perfection is worth reaching for, but failure to attain it shouldn't be cause for despair. For in perfection there is no action, no need for it, and without action there is no life. If all conflict was resolved by turning of the other cheek, there would be no conflict and no story and no life. There is little danger that this will occur, and Jesus's advice to turn the cheek is excellent for the individual, but disappointment over lack of perfection may well be tempered by joy in active life.

While it is widely recognized that imperfection is implicit in the human condition, it is perhaps less universally understood that acceptance of that imperfection is

paradoxically, a kind of completeness. When a person realizes that he is flawed and incomplete and dependent upon all that exists for his possible—and, since death completes, inevitable—perfection, and accepts that condition as what is and what is going to be and what must be and even what should be, the experience he has is one that may match in freedom and ecstasy that of perfection itself.

Because no man is complete, the physician cannot heal himself. The impossibility of his doing so is understandable in terms of Groddeck's medicine, for it is obvious that no person can serve as a catalyst for himself. A person can love himself, and in some sense should do so, but to limit oneself to self-love is to damn oneself to a descent into the hell of one's own imperfections magnified. Understanding this, the Judoka, despite his own considerable abilities in healing, asks Leeda to serve as his physician. She does not need to know a great deal about procedures. She needs only to love, and this she already does.

The Judoka, who knows the ecstasy of acceptance of his own flaws and of acceptance of the world as it is, who knows the value of human exchange and participates in it, and who communicates with other people as fully as anyone can, is nevertheless subject to great loneliness.

He has known a period in which he was more totally and continually alone than he is now. He was what Colin Wilson calls an *Outsider*, a person who sees "too far and too deep" and therefore beyond what seems to ordinary men the order of the world. He sees into the abyss on the far side.

In Wilson's schematic notion, a baby is born into chaos, but as he matures he begins to see the world as ordered. This is the order that the average man, the Insider, sees. But the Outsider sees beyond. He views the activities of men, even eating and reproducing and dying, *as beside the point* (although he does not know quite what the point is). The Outsider feels that somewhere, somehow, there is something that is not beside the point; that there exists something of value and that he may be able to find it. Some Outsiders do find it. They find it implicit in existence itself. By coming intensely alive, as one does when in crisis or near death or in love or in any peak experience, they see that it is *meaning* that is beside the point, that meaning and existence are the same thing. When the Outsider reaches this stage, he sees a new kind of order. Now nothing is important, for no one thing has more significance than everything else around it; in other words, everything is important. For everything is, and in that *isness* is value. By no means is the order seen on this level to be identified with the order seen by the Insider. The world is the same, yet it is altogether different. The *kind* of order has changed. The Judoka has reached this state—"beyond the Outsider" in Wilson's phrase.

But if a man's true being is not just what we conventionally identify as his body but is everything that exists (and all our records of enlightenment experience suggest that the situation looks this way from that perspective), then all strength must be compensated for by weakness, for the strength must be drawn from somewhere. The Judoka has no great strength in any particular aspect:

his great strength is in his general handling of all that arises. Correspondingly, his weakness is general. It takes the form of seeing too far again, of seeing too clearly the horror that is the other side of joy and that with joy seems to pervade the deepest reaches into which man can see. It is as if the Judoka goes to still another level and peers off the edge of another abyss. He knows now that the succession of levels is probably an infinite regress, and so this one does not affect him quite as the Outsider's level does the Outsider. An infinite regress is itself a form of order. Still, this abyss makes the Judoka acutely and terribly of his own separateness, which is a frightening thing. This is what he calls vastation; it is the other side of ecstasy. Judoka can accept it, but he feels an ultimate weakness.

The Judoka would not return to a lower level even if he but he recognizes that to move past any level is to lose comfort. And the loss is real.

Because there is no winning and no changing anything, reality appears to be so vast and indefinable that anything believed is an image of the truth, there is really nothing to teach and nothing to learn (although teaching and learning are part of the game and have value as all aspects of life have value). As Kierkegaard points out, all one can do finally is stand in silence. This, clearly, is true prayer—standing in silence and awe and appreciation of it all. I use the word *appreciation* in the sense that one *appreciates* a literary work: becomes immersed in it, experiences it, participates in it, wonders at it.

Robert Musil's Man Without Qualities has a street fight and then declares that "boxing is theology." Silence before the gods is one mode of appreciation, but activity is another, and strife and love are the two poles of action. Both strife and love function in many ways that justify the designation theology, but one function of strife requires special mention here. In crisis one comes more fully alive than at most other times. This is at least part of the appeal of parachute jumping, for example. When one brushes death, life becomes infinitely sweet. To a man long in the desert, beer and Coke are beside the point; simple, unadulterated water is the essence of delight. Any peak experience may provide a similar effect, but the crisis of conflict provides at the same time a taste of the terror of existence. This tasting of the sweetness of life, of its joy, but also of its bitterness, is a breakthrough to reality, contact with what is or the divine. It is a communion with the gods and it results in a knowledge-by-acquaintance of them. In this sense, then, fighting is theology.

知

The next morning both the man and the woman sleep late. After making coffee, Leeda, seeing that there are no more provisions, decides to go to her hotel, get some money, and shop for groceries.

"What would you do," she asks, "if you were hurt and couldn't hunt and there was no one here to go buy food?"

"Fast, I guess," the Judoka replies. Apparently the prospect would not alarm him. As Leeda leaves, the Judoka asks her to stop by the boy's house and get him to walk up to the enclosure. "Tell him I need him," he says.

"Are you sure you feel like taking care of him?" the woman asks.

"I want him to take care of me: be sort of a back-up physician on the case," the Judoka answers.

Leeda searches his face for a sign that he is teasing, but there is none. She leaves. When she returns with the boy, she finds the Judoka lying on his back with his hands folded behind his head, apparently lost in thought.

"What are you doing?" she asks.

He grins. "Making some plans for another show," he says.

"I thought you always lived in the present, never making plans," the woman says. She is half teasing, but only half: she has not seen him take much thought for the future.

The Judoka stretches his arms. "Planning is an activity just like anything else. It can be enjoyed for its own sake, and occasionally it's helpful—provided you never expect your plans to work out in the form in which you make them. It's not a thing one ought to do all the time."

Now the Judoka turns his attention to the boy. He tells the boy the story of the fight and shows him the resultant cuts and bruises, describing in detail the soreness and stiffness and weakness of various parts of his body. Then the Judoka explains to the boy that healing is at least in part a matter of exchange and that since it is, and since no one can very well exchange strengths with himself one must rely on other people for assistance in regaining strength.

The boy sees what the Judoka has in mind, and he objects: how can he give strength to the Judoka when the Judoka, despite his injuries, is still far stronger than the boy? The man explains that the boy's lack of soreness, his flexibility where he himself has stiffness, is a kind of strength, and that, besides, the relative quantity of strength is rather beside the point: the boy has some strength, and that is all that is important. The boy nods. The Judoka explains the exchange he wants to take place—a massage, in which the boy lets his strength flow into the man and the man's weakness flow into the boy.

Leeda objects. She sends the boy on a short errand outside the enclosure and addresses the Judoka: This boy can't stand any more weakness than he already has. She herself is not at all certain that she takes any of this seriously, but just in case—

The man overrules the objection, explaining that the kinds of weakness that will flow are only those that correspond to the boy's strengths; therefore the boy will not be hurt. Besides, he adds, the boy can release only that strength of which he has a surplus.

The boy returns, impatient to start. The Judoka, however, is not quite ready. He has more instruction to give. He explains to the boy about what the aikidomen call *ki*—vitality, life, the stuff of which the universe was formed, that which must constantly flow into and out of a person as long as he lives. The aikidomen, he continues, think that one can encourage this flow by consciously letting ki flow in and out. Also, he says, they demonstrate this flow (especially to themselves) by letting it enable them to do things with their bodies that they could not otherwise do. In this way also, he concludes, they instruct themselves in the art of letting ki flow.

This is what the Judoka wants to do now: let the boy instruct himself in and master the art of letting ki flow. The Judoka tells the boy that the aikidomen believe that they can make an arm unbendable by picturing it as a firehose with ki flooding through. In this fashion they can make an arm unbendable—or very difficult to bend—without consciously or apparently tensing any muscles at all! The Judoka asks the boy to try it. The boy does. The Judoka asks the woman to try the arm. Do not hold back at all, he instructs her.

As soon as the woman starts to push, the boy tenses his arm and Leeda bends it rather easily. Finally, after several tries, he sighs and more or less gives up. But when he quits trying with his muscles he captures the image, and surprisingly to him and to the young woman, his arm becomes a little harder to push. On repeated efforts (or, more precisely, non-efforts) the arm grows harder and harder for the woman to bend. After a while, the boy says he has it. The Judoka tells him that this same flowing of ki, now through both arms and hands, is what should be maintained throughout the massage.

When the boy leaves, some two hours later, both he and the Judoka seem to be feeling much better than they did when the project started. Leeda is not at all sure what she thinks.

Late in the afternoon, the Judoka does some yoga stretches, gingerly and awkwardly, and then a few very light calisthenics. The boy does little at home, but spends one of the happier afternoons of his life just reflecting on what he has done. The only thing that has marred his day was the ugly expression on the face of a redhaired man who was watching the Judoka's enclosure when the boy left.


Two days later, the Judoka, having done a good bit of stretching and walking and swimming, is ready to give the girl another judo lesson.

As usual, the lesson begins with stretches, warm-up, and the ceremonial bows, followed by a session of ukemi. Then they go into the dance exercise in which one responds by pulling with the other's pushes, pushing with the other's pulls, and moving one's ankles in the directions of pressures from the insides of the other's feet. Leeda occasionally takes the initiative and tries to push or pull too quickly for the Judoka to make a response. At this, she is not quite so able as the Judoka, but in responding she is still a little better, a touch more graceful, than he is. After all the rehearsals for the show, the exercise has become a real and highly pleasurable dance. The couple—and they are a couple in this exercise, for their every motion is not separate but united—continue it far longer than would be permitted in a rigidly controlled practice session. When they close their eyes and go into blind randori, this drill seems but a heightened and deepened form of the dance. Leeda falls so smoothly that she actually enjoys being thrown. She has overcome her repugnance against throwing—the result, probably, of an inhibition against hurting anything—and now throws so smoothly that the Judoka can enjoy her throws.

Finally tiring of this exercise, they move to instruction in and practice of throwing and holding techniques. He shows her *okuri-ashi-harai*, a double foot sweep, in which a person places the sole of his foot outside his adversary's ankle and moves it to the inside, sweeping both feet out from under. He tells her that this throw can be successful only with near-perfect timing. In order to let her practice the timing, he sets up another dance. In this one the partners catch hands and skip sideways four or five paces, on any one of which Tori—the person throwing—sweeps the feet out from under Uke. This dance has a certain lilt to it.

Later the Judoka shifts to *ushiro-goshi*, rear loin throw, which is a counter to a throw like o-goshi. When attacked by o-goshi, he tells his student, one may simply step lightly aside and bend with the throw so that the body does not go up and over, and then, when the adversary relaxes for an instant after his unsuccessful throwing attempt, catch him around the middle and lift as he is straightening up. Having his feet off the ground, one can fairly easily deposit him as desired.

Leeda practices both of these throws, falling into an appropriate holddown with the completion of each successful maneuver. For the ushiro-goshi and okuri-ashi-harai tactics, she

192

uses a holding technique called *yoko-shiho-gatame*, which takes advantage of easy access to the fallen adversary's undefended side and prevents his rising by gentle shifting of weight to meet pressures from him.

After the throws the Judoka takes up again the ju-no-kata, and again he lays great stress on the matter of letting the adversary throw himself. Following the ju-no-kata, the Judoka and his partner try some straight (i.e. not blind) randori. Then the Judoka decides to take advantage of his weakened condition and let the girl try some *shiai*—actual contest. She does not come close to winning, but the contest is more nearly even than it could be were the Judoka not sore, stiff, and weakened. The shiai is valuable for the young woman, for in it she gets a taste of the excitement and value of actual conflict.

Shiai would normally end a lesson, except for a few "cooling off" calisthenics, but the Judoka has one more thing on his mind on this occasion. He recalls to the woman his conversation with the boy about aikido and the flow of ki; he points out that these metaphors of aikido have great value for the judoman in that they help him to set and maintain a posture appropriate to effective judo. He has her try the unbendable arm exercise. Like the boy, she has to try it many times before she is successful, but finally she manages to do it; like the boy she finds the achievement highly exciting. The Judoka then tells her about the Oriental practice of "thinking with the stomach" and of the value of this practice in maintaining balance, effective low center of gravity, and maneuverability. The aikidoman thinks with his stomach, the Judoka says, by relating the inner and outer flow of ki to inhalation and exhalation directed to and from a point about four inches below the navel. He has Leeda practice this exercise also. In concluding the lesson, he tells her about the aikidoman's highest art: directing the ki of the adversary so that no fight is necessary—much as a person who loves dogs can direct the ki of an angry dog. He has already demonstrated this maneuver, both successfully and unsuccessfully.

知

The Judoka manages to enjoy almost everything he does. One reason is that he seeks out the enjoyable way of doing whatever it is. When he wants or needs to do anything, he does not blindly imitate what he has previously seen done. Rather, he thinks of the desired result and then tries to figure out an effective and enjoyable way of achieving it. Very often he comes up with a way that stimulates an aesthetic response—a *poetic method* of doing the job.

His experience with the boy is enjoyable for both himself and the boy. The massage is valuable to the Judoka for exactly the reasons he gives, although perhaps not in the exact sense in which the boy understands those reasons. The giving of the massage is also valuable to the boy, as Leeda recognizes.

The judo practice is also enjoyable, and when the Judoka finds an aspect of that practice that is especially enjoyable— in this instance the dance merging into the blind randori—he lets it run its course. I suspect that a serious weakness of much judo done in American dojos results from too much puritan work ethic on the part of students and instructors: there is too much practicing judo and not enough playing judo. That is, there is too much sacrifice of the present to the future, too much working for belts or contest trophies or future status as an expert, too little doing of judo for simple delight of the moment. This situation has an adverse effect, not only on the general lives of the students, but on the actual learning of judo. Far more American boys are expert at baseball than at piano. No doubt the main reason for this is relative difficulty; but it also may be that boys *have to practice* the piano and then are *permitted to go out and play* baseball.

George B. Leonard argues in Education and Ecstasy that all education is ecstatic; that is, whenever excitement is lacking *there is no learning going on*. Learning is change, he writes, and change is exciting. On this basis he argues that the many minutes of dull class through which the average American child sits are not educative at all but actually deadening. I think that Leonard is correct and that we as a people had better reorganize our schools or else close them down altogether. When true learning is going on, the student feels delight (or he suffers, but if he suffers the suffering itself is exciting) as the boy does when he makes the unbendable arm exercise work. This excitement ending in delight might well be our test of any educational program, as enjoyability might well serve as a test for the food we eat and the exercise we take.

This notion may or may not meet the criteria of "common sense," depending upon how one looks at it; but it is closer to it than the Judoka's esoteric doctrines of exchange and flow-of-ki.

The Judoka has a good many beliefs that are at variance with the dictates of common sense. He does not have that complete contempt for popular wisdom that some people take as the mark of intellectuality, for if whatever can be believed is at least a distorted image of the truth, popular wisdom has within its muddy waters some reflection of reality. But neither does he have any great respect for the mass view; that a notion is widely held tends more to make him question it than to make him accept it.

Neither does the Judoka have that contempt for analytic logic adopted by some people who experience poetry and who begin to have some respect for the paradoxical logic of the East. Nor yet does he have the converse—the superstitious regard for that special brand of academic logic that was for many years the supposed distinguishing characteristic of thinkers in the West. He takes both analytical and paradoxical reason as guides in thinking, but he makes no decision on the basis of either of these acting alone or, ordinarily, even of both of them acting in concert. When he is presented with an idea, he applies his reason— in all of its forms he knows that have a feel of truth—to the idea, and then he applies to it the test of aesthetic response: does it feel right and does it work well in his As If *Weltanschauung*.

The Judoka both intuits and intellectualizes. There is an old dichotomy suggesting that a person must be either a man of letters—i.e. of the intellect—or a man of action who depends upon his intuition. For this dichotomy there is some excuse in experience. The quality of imagination, which is indispensable in the man of intellect (or for that matter in the person who is fully human), is in certain respects a liability for the man of action. But to decide on the basis of this principle that one must choose between a life of thought and one of action is to ignore the possibility that a man of intellect may learn to suspend his imagination and to weigh into his decisions the suggestions of intuition. Certainly we do have examples of people who were or are at once men of intellect and of action: Christopher Marlowe and Walter Raleigh and the explorer Richard Burton and Lawrence of Arabia and Camus and Sartre and Malraux, to name a few. While the Judoka has not the accomplishments of these men and may never have, he is of their class insofar as his life is one of both thought and action.

The Judoka can consider and sometimes give credence to esoteric ways of healing or knowing or acting because he makes fewer and less restrictive assumptions about the nature of reality than do most people. He is somewhat in the position of Carlos Castaneda, the young anthropologist who, because he could suspend ordinary "civilized" or "enlightened" judgments about what is real, was able to discover through a Yaqui Indian sorcerer a believable system of non-ordinary reality. It is impossible to exaggerate the significance of Castaneda's experience: first, because it demonstrates that the world is not nearly as simple as nineteenth-century science thought and that the despairing judgments on it were premature; second, because it makes possible the reordering of reality now that the order we have threatens to become unworkable; third, because it makes awe easier, silence before the gods, worship and appreciation that are the only true forms of self-improvement.

Pearce's *The Crack in the Cosmic Egg* formulates an assumption about the nature of reality that—while itself embodying a metaphor, so far as I can tell—comes as close as anything I know to describing reality itself as a kind of metaphor and therefore not a thing or a collection of things at all as we ordinarily use that term. Pearce argues that "our reality is influenced by our notions *about* reality, regardless of the nature of those notions" and that "there is a relationship between what we *think* is out there in the world and what we experience as being out there" and that "our looking enters as one of the determinants in the reality event that we see." On these bases he moves to William Blake's claim that perception is the universal, the perceived object the particular. "*What* is discovered by man is never the 'universal' or cosmic 'truth,' " Pearce explains. "Rather, the *process* by which the mind brings about a 'discovery' is itself the 'universal.' " Pearce's *cosmic egg* is the sum total of our notions about what reality is. The *crack* is Pearce's mode of thinking through which imagination can escape to create a new cosmic egg. It gives man a chance to "seize the tiller of the world" as Teilhard de Chardin put it. In other words, it is a way of shaping reality.

To suggest that a person can shape his own (or the world's) reality is not to suggest that he is free to shape it any way he pleases. I doubt, for example, that any shaping would enable one to get beyond the seesaw principle. There may be a few absolutes.

A question arises as to whether or not reshaping reality is worthwhile, even if it is possible, for in reshaping it one is about as likely to do a poor job as to do a good one—more likely, unless one's poetic consciousness is highly developed. Still, if reality is shapable, is malleable, that malleability is one of its qualities and is therefore a proper subject for knowing; and if this is one of its principal qualities the study of it may be the vehicle for one of the highest forms of knowing. If so, one may well attempt some reshaping of reality just in order to know, for knowing is the way of genuine appreciation.

The Judoka delves only slightly into the matter of shaped reality with his use of yogic devices and exchange and flow-of-ki. He makes only small cracks in the cosmic egg, and he makes even those cautiously. Nevertheless, he demonstrates how even a very practical art can be used to experiment with cracking techniques.

知

One day when Leeda arrives at the enclosure the Judoka very calmly requests that she take off her bathing suit. She is surprised, and, looking at the man, she is certain that at the moment sex is not what he has in mind; but she cannot guess what he does intend. Nevertheless, she does as he asks, and she is delighted to observe that his penis is stirring beneath his bathing trunks. She feels with pleasure her own vulnerability and a desire stirring within herself. She looks at him quizzically, smiling gently. Repressed excitement fills the air.

"Lie down, here on the sleeping bag," he says. "On your stomach."

The Judoka kneels beside her. He touches her ankle, and then runs his hands lightly over her legs, her buttocks, her back and arms and shoulders and neck.

The Judoka stops and chuckles. "We're getting just the opposite effect to the one I want. I want you to relax."

Leeda laughs. "Do you really think this is going to do it?"

His voice is grave when he next speaks. "Yes, I do. But we have to overcome the excitement that arises from our being of different sexes. The current stirred by that difference can be valuable to us— I mean even here in the massage—if we can go beyond it into a kind of repose."

He lays open palms against her thigh and her buttock. In a few seconds they give her an impression of being hands without feeling, inert masses of flesh, hands of a man unaware that what he is touching is a woman.

He begins to talk, his voice a low monotone: "Picture me as a kindly, old family doctor, who wants only to let you fully relax . . . Let the muscles of your left calf relax . . . Don't help them, don't make them, just let them . . ."

The human being who is sensitive and honest and alive, is in some sense ageless: always at once man and boy or woman and girl, inside and out. Leeda is such a person, and now, as subject in this uncommon affair, seems to herself predominantly girl.

Again the man's hands begin to move over her body, his monotone instructions continuing. The girl slips into a light trance as the hands now seem to induce repose wherever they touch. The quietness and calmness of the repose is delicious. In the back of her mind, Leeda is aware that she has not for many years known such complete relaxation. She is reminded of the first time she rode in an airplane, and of how at the beginning she refused to put her whole weight down into the seat, and of how she finally came to trust the plane and to let herself sink into the seat. Her repose now has that quality relative to her normal life.

But after a while the massage changes. It becomes harder and rougher. The girl loses her picture of the kindly, old family doctor and sees instead in her mind's eye a now-silent Judoka. She wonders if he is angry.

He kneads the muscle at the back of her neck. It feels good, yet after a while it almost hurts. Her emotions begin to play tricks. She wants to cry. Finally she sinks into an abyss of melancholy. She can no longer control the urge. She does cry.

"I'm sorry," she says, sobbing.

"Don't be sorry," the Judoka says. "You are doing exactly what I hoped you would do."

She lets herself go then and cries as she has not cried since she was a little girl.

The Judoka turns her over and begins to work on her chest. For an instant she is aware of her breasts, but she loses that awareness almost immediately as her melancholy grows even deeper and then develops into a kind of longing—the deep longing of nostalgia, the feeling of a person who has been away from the sea since early childhood and then gets a breath of salt air. It is a kind of heartbreak. The man's hands move to the girl's face, in the vicinity of her eyes, and the nostalgia grows heavier. Again she sobs.

His hands move back down around the chest, and what has been a longing becomes a kind of hostility. Leeda grows angry at the Judoka and at the world. His hands move down to the diaphragm, and old, remembered angers begin to pass before the girl's eyes. She is intensely aware of the Judoka's hands and of some mysterious connection between them and the emotions she is experiencing. She feels as if she were wearing her soul on the outside. Despite her awareness, she can do nothing about what is happening. Her anger darkens. It grows into a murderous rage.

"Hit the sand if you feel angry," the Judoka says.

The girl does. She strikes the ground time and time again until her hands sting. She doesn't care. She is hurting, killing, and she lets go: she kills, kills, kills! She is exhausted.

The Judoka's hands move to her pelvic area, and she feels anxiety, fear of him and hatred of him. Her mind is curiously two minds. In one of them she knows that the Judoka is doing all of this deliberately and that he is doing it for her. But in that mind she knows also what is happening in the other mind. There she is afraid—afraid of penetration by this man whom she knows she loves, afraid of all men in the world, afraid of masculinity itself, afraid even of God, whom she can't help but picture as masculinity heightened and intensified wanting to possess her and enter her and destroy her. She envisions the great penis of the world as a snake fascinating and frightening beyond the outer limits of conception.

Throughout herself she feels split, and anger at herself for being split, and rage at the world for splitting her. She feels messy and awkward and dirty and ashamed. She feels naked and cheap and as if her soul is on the outside and is too horrifying to be seen. She feels moments of pure, black terror. Then she sinks into a despair. The despair sinks and sinks and sinks. She wants to die, but dying would require too great an effort. Her soul, still on the outside, is now a swarm of maggots. She hates and despises everything that exists, herself most of all. A great nausea seizes her. The Judoka takes his hands from her, and she knows that he does so in repugnance. Through her mind passes the phrase, "the dark night of the soul." She wishes that she had never come to this place or met this man.

The Judoka turns her over again, so that her stomach is to the ground. Once again, the quality of his hands changes, and now he is talking again, quietly and calmly. His hands feel almost like soap, or a soapy brush, cleansing her as they move across her body. The hands move briskly and vigorously, yet they have about them a suggestion of caress.

Slowly, the despair and the terror and the horror and the fear and the anxiety and the degradation and the heartbreak and the anger and the darkness ball up into a large and then a smaller ball. Her whole person is that ball. It shrinks smaller and smaller, more and more concentrated. Her muscles tense and contract; she becomes smaller. As the ball sucks itself in and reduces in size again and again it changes color and tone; it transforms itself into a seed. She becomes a seed. And now she feels within her a stirring of life and she knows in an instant what it must feel like to be an expectant mother—but in this case she is both the pregnant one and that with which she is pregnant.

The Judoka's hands now move gently and expansively. She seems to grow again, shooting up long and slim and strong and supple. She opens out at intervals, broad and flat and receptive, shading and cooling and watering herself.

Again the Judoka turns her onto her back. Again she is aware of her breasts, but now the pink nipples seem like buds and she is proud of them. Her body surrounds and protects them and gives them emphasis. Her arms and legs are the petals of her breasts. Again she feels a stirring as of motherhood and an awareness that her womb will bear fruit. For a moment she wonders if she has been hypnotized and the Judoka has entered her. But the wonder is a pleasurable curiosity—not even a curiosity, really, for she knows that he has not—and a consciousness that, if he has, fine, for now the womb will bear fruit.

Now the girl moves slightly at the Judoka's guiding touch, and as she settles into a new position on her back she knows that she is no longer in any kind of trance. She is more fully conscious than she has ever been, and the sky is a richer blue. The Judoka's hands move over her, caressing like water, and she breathes through them as if she had gills. His touch is alive, and her body is alive, and she is now intensely sexual: she is responsive woman in every part of her being. She is immersed in his hands and wants to drown in them, in a delightful drowning; but she doesn't drown, she becomes more and more alive to his touch. She is conscious too of the salt air, and her nostrils quiver at the scent like an animal's, and she wants to run with the graceful gait of a fine doe to the source of the scent. She can almost taste the air, and her body seems to hover and sample the salt air and the blue sky and the man's hands and the man's mouth. And now her ears come alive and she listens to the music of the waves and the muffled roar of distant trucks and from not far off the occasional sound of crickets. Her ears almost literally pick up in the manner of a she-wolf, and like a she-wolf she feels at once feminine and strong and dangerous. She feels a quiet and powerful ecstasy. If only she could stay like this forever!

But already the Judoka is doing new things. He lifts her leg a little and lets it fall, and then he lifts and lets fall the flesh of her thigh. He stretches her arms and then has her stretch them and then has her arch and stretch her back. Catlike, she arches and pulls and delights in the full, graceful feeling of her whole self. She sees now into the rich blueness of the heavens, and her eyes like giant wings carry her through them, soaring and sailing.

Now it all comes together and she is a girl and a woman and a person. A person, but beyond a person: she is a goddess. The sky and the ground and the salt air and the man's hands and the man himself are parts of her. She includes them. They are parts of her body as if she were Mother Nature.

Yet in an instant there is nothing there but the blue sky and the sea breeze and the man. She herself is nothing; she is a void. But this is equally delighting. She is still a goddess or at least a water nymph. In her nothingness she is everything.

Now all thought of herself and all else bubbles off. At once a goddess and a plant, she is nothing and everything, and she is silent before the gods. Her being is all senses and responses. She is fully alive and fully relaxed and fully excited; and there is no contradiction among these states, no interference of one with another. She is utterly and completely a person of the present and in love with it.

"Sleep now," the Judoka says. "I'll watch over you."

When she awakens she finds it easy to pretend that she is Milton's Eve new come to the Garden.

知

Lyrical experience is available to anyone who is sufficiently free to claim it, who is willing to suffer the pain that accompanies it, who finds a means of access to it, and who has the will or the assistance to drive through to it. It is of course poetry. Poetry, like theology and experiment, is a way of cracking the cosmic egg, a way of knowing.

"Encounter" is a term we hear fairly often now. It started out as the name for a therapy, but the therapy quite naturally developed into an educational device also, and the term now gives a name to a process that serves both functions at once. The idea is simply that genuine communication and exchange between human beings facilitates beneficial change in them.

Judo itself involves encounter and exchange, as we see most clearly in the push-pull exercise. Massage, another vehicle for encounter and exchange, is the antithesis of judo but nevertheless a form of it, a way of taking the other person where he wants to go. As shiai is a limited expression of war, massage is a limited expression of love.

Because it is both a symbolic and a literal disclosure of the whole self, including those parts that are usually kept hidden, nudity is an important aspect of encounter. It is worth noting both that nudity has value and that it loses its value if it is overused. Nudity has value as disclosure, just as it has erotic value, only if it is an occasional rather than a constant thing. It is essential to massage on the further ground that it permits access to the person.

Massage is an ancient therapy, long neglected, and like hypnosis, left for the most part to charlatans. Also like hypnosis, it is beginning to make a comeback. Massage has value for several reasons, not the least of which is the encounter it provides between physician and patient. (I suspect this is one reason for Groddeck's use of it.) That encounter may be verbal—before or during or after the massage—but it must be non-verbal, through the laying on of hands, the sense of touch. It may be that encounter-by-touch is an especially valuable activity in our culture, which traditionally starves people of communication by touch.

The Judoka admits that his massage of the nude girl is an erotic activity. But the erotic in itself is neither good nor bad; it becomes one or the other according to the attitudes of the people engaging in the activity. The mutual attraction of man and woman facilitates exchange and communication, for that very reason cross-sexual massage, properly handled, is probably more effective as encounter than man-on-man or woman-on-woman, in which many people must overcome a repugnance to what seems almost a homosexual engagement. Either kind i.e. regardless of the sexual make-up of the partnership—to be effective would seem to require doing what the Judoka himself does and instructs Leeda to do: imaginatively reconstruct the scene so as to move the sexual element to the back of the mind, out of the way so to speak.

Massage has another value in that it may serve to de-armor the character. "Character Armor" is Wilhelm Reich's term. Reich's idea is that every person develops a character armor of the body that precisely parallels the form of the inner man. It works something like this: If a person is usually buoyant, he holds his shoulders one way; if he is usually despondent, he holds them another. The set of his shoulders has an effect on his chest cavity and on his abdominal organs and ultimately on everything else in his body including his muscle tone. So, Reich argues, it is with all the characteristics of the person—all of them are expressed in the body. The resultant bad tone of the muscles (insofar as it is bad) and the way in which the musculature works to the disadvantage of the person—as in inhibiting his ability to cry, for example—is the character armor. Reich's concept is analogous to the fictional convention of paralleling bodily and mental and spiritual qualities. It is an expression of William Blake's doctrine that the body is but that portion of the soul discernible by the five senses. It is a development of Lavater's and Goethe's idea that the external form of man is an expression of his soul. But Reich goes further: He believed that if we can learn to read accurately the language of the body we can know everything there is to know about a person. He also believed that one can *treat the psyche through the body*; that by rendering flexible the character armor one can contribute to the opening up and consequent healing of the psyche. In a way, what Reich does corresponds to the old first-grade-teacher practice of telling the children that they will feel better if they turn up the corners of their mouths. Reichian therapy is a sophisticated and profound development of the principle involved there.

De-armoring is what the Judoka is doing when he massages in such ways that the woman is virtually forced to give way and give expression to long pent up emotions of sadness and anger and despair. The pain of letting go is an early effect of character de-armoring and an essential one to the later release into full freedom. Probably it would be unusual (and perhaps too exhausting) for a person to go through the whole cycle in one massage, but I show it that way simply as a suggestion of what can happen. Certainly the Judoka never goes further in a single session than the patient is ripe for, since it is his business only to help the patient to free himself, not to force or even induce the patient into some preconceived mold of the Judoka's design.

That this massage causes the young woman intense suffering does not render massage inconsistent with the Judoka's Ways of doing other things—that is, of doing them in a fashion in which the process itself is enjoyable. The suffering of this letting go differs in quality from the kind of suffering that results from damage to the person and that indicates one should change one's actions. The suffering of the letting go is intense and miserable, but it has about it the quality of value in itself such that, if no "beneficial" result ensued, the experience itself would be recognized as worthwhile. The pain is similar to that of pressure on a boil that has come to a head and demands explosive release: the pain "feels good." For this reason as well as because it deals with the person as a whole and because it changes consciousness, massage, even character de-armoring massage, is a *poetic method* of therapy and education, of human development.

*Scientific method* is a familiar term in our culture. It refers, of course, to the process of controlled empirical observation subjected to analytical reasoning and leading to the abstraction of general laws. Our civilization has used scientific method to good advantage, but it seems now to have overdone dependence on it: in isolating parts—i.e. fragmenting, the necessary consequence of analysis—we have often neglected the whole. It is for this reason that we now have the ecological crisis on our hands. We are now coming to see that we have unnecessarily restricted our point of view and thereby understood less about the world around us than we might have.

The time seems ripe to explore the possibility of developing a comparable *poetic method*, a Poet's Way of approaching that which is without as well as that which is within the sphere of the fine arts. Such a poetic method would start its investigation (i.e., its knowing) or its modification (i.e., its doing) of anything by looking at the entire subject and background rather than by immediately tearing apart. It would consider the whole in all observation and manipulation, in the manner of the ecologist. It would consider aesthetic response on the same level and of the same significance as logical validity. It would be less concerned with achieving knowledge or control than with achieving "life more abundant"—or rather, it would be concerned with knowledge and control principally insofar as they lead to that goal. Such a poetic method would include scientific method as a constituent, as synthesis includes analysis.

We already have a foundation upon which to build this poetic method: judo itself—the poetic way. Judo is a poetic method of handling conflict and of being. Simple extension and modification make it a general poetic method.

In a way, this whole book is simply an elaboration of this concept of poetic method. The Judoka is a man who attempts to apply poetic method to his being, his knowing, and his doing. Judo as a fighting art is nothing but a way of loving the adversary and of expressing that love in an ironic and aesthetically satisfying manner; thus, it is a poetic method of fighting. As that, it is by extension a poetic method of loving. Aleister Crowley's treatment of mosquitoes by loving them is a poetic way of handling a nuisance; so is G. K. Chesterton's attitude toward inconvenience. Huxley's way of chewing grace is poetic method in action, as is the Zen swordsman's no-mind way of fighting. Veisser's paradoxical theory of change suggests a poetic method of handling bad habits. My notion, following Vahinger, of As If *Weltanschauung* and the yoga and aikido use of metaphor are poetic ways of inducing new ones. Groddeck's medicine—and Jesus's—are poetic methods of healing. So is Reich's breaking of the character armor. The Judoka's method of teaching by exchange is a poetic way of teaching (and learning). Pearce's cracking of the cosmic egg is a poetic method of knowing, especially when it culminates in any of the extremes of being: Kierkegaard's silence before God or Musil's conflict as theology or Charles Williams's exchange in human love.

Perhaps the chief modern proponent of poetic method in that field in which on first thought it might seem least useful, empirical science itself, is Johann Wolfgang von Goethe. I say "perhaps" because I'm not at all certain that Einstein's imaginative use of trains and lights and Freud's metaphoric construct of man and use of myth do not make those men users of poetic method. However that may be, Goethe not only used poetic method but recognized that he was using it and theorized about it. Goethe's scientific achievements have been underrated—he is usually regarded merely as a forerunner of Darwin and a kind of curiosity, a poet who was also a serious man of science—not because his findings were wrong but because he was too far ahead of his time.

Rudolf Steiner—himself no mean user of poetic method in science—quotes Goethe as saying: "Reason deals with the becoming, the intellect with the already become; the former does not trouble to ask: What for? The latter does not ask: From what? The former rejoices in the state of evolving; the latter wishes to hold everything fast in order to use it." By *reason* here Goethe seems to mean some kind of thought process in poetic intuition as distinguished from *intellect*, by which he seems to mean abstract analytical power. He appears to use the term *reason* in the same way in this statement: "Reason holds rule only over the living; therefore the world that has come into existence, with which geognosy deals, is dead." Goethe makes a similar point in admiringly describing a teaching hospital in Rome, saying that in German medical-surgical anatomy only knowledge of the part is important, while to the Italians *the parts signify nothing unless they at the same time reveal a noble, beautiful form.* "Thus it is customary also," Goethe writes, "after the example of the ancients, to study the skeleton, not as an artificially assembled bony mass, but rather together with the ligaments by means of which it acquires life and movement."

Goethe shows by his words—and Steiner shows by his citing of them—consciousness of that s*pirit*, that mood and tone, which is the essence of poetic method. It is an almost ecstatic spirit that combines high seriousness with something very near playfulness. This spirit constitutes and gives rise to (in a cyclic relation) that *element of the enjoyable* in poetic method that makes possible equal stress on means and ends. The mood comes through in descriptions of Goethe's entire career. It is one of those factors that joined Goethe's art and his science.

The joining of art and science is itself a principal mark of poetic method. Steiner devotes a whole chapter of his *Goethe the Scientist* to an argument that Goethe the poet and Goethe the thinker are related, not in separate inclinations that just happen to be combined in one personality, but in a view of art and science as coming from a single source—of art and science coming into contact in such a way that perfection in one field requires perfection in the other.

Goethe usually initiated his researches with an aesthetically satisfying idea of the whole field. Then he modified his idea as he made discoveries, or, more often, directed his inquiries toward gaps in factual knowledge that when filled in confirmed the idea of the whole. It was in this latter manner that he discovered the intermaxillary bone in the human being. And through working with an aesthetically satisfying idea of the whole he saw in the leaf the basic form of the plant. By conducting his researches in this manner, he conformed to two basic elements in poetic method: working with wholes and achieving and judging radiance.

To inquire with an idea in mind is, of course, a dangerous procedure, for it may lead one to overvalue one kind of information and undervalue another in order to make the facts fit the theory. It may thus cost one *objectivity*; and, indeed, it is because later science has worshipped objectivity that much of Goethe's work has been ignored. But what those critics of Goethe fail to realize is that the very notion that objectivity is possible is itself an idea of the whole—one that is just as dangerous as any idea of Goethe's and a great deal less satisfying aesthetically than most of his. The danger of Goethe's brand of poetic method is offset by a refusal to make a superstition of the idea of the whole or of any discoveries already made or any theory already confirmed; in other words, by a realization that all is becoming and that becoming continues to become, that nothing, including knowledge, is static. A researcher who refuses to idolize either objectivity or his own idea of the whole is in excellent position to plunge to the very heart of what is. I can't help but add that, in view of Pearce's way of regarding man's participation in the construction of reality, a scientist of Goethe's quality might be of inestimable value in *making reality itself poetic*!

Goethe's career reveals a critical point concerning any man who would live and work and know by means of poetic method. There has always been confusion about what Goethe "was"—a poet or a public man or a botanist or what. The truth is that he was all of these things and none of them: we cannot say that he was any of them, even a poet, because the verb to be sets up an equation and Goethe was more than a poet. So it must be with the *field poet*—i.e., one who applies poetic method to the whole field of human activity (or "out of the field" so to speak). It has to be this way because the poetic method requires letting the process ripen and work in its own way, and therefore one cannot fit into any preconceived mold. Say for example, that a person wants to be a writer. If he is going to apply poetic method to his writing, he cannot force anything—he must wait for whatever he has to say to ripen in him and stir and demand to emerge, like a baby from the womb. Until he has that something to say in its ripeness he cannot be a writer. Until that time he must do whatever is ripe for him. He can have no real profession. He must be, like Goethe, simply a man. But perhaps that is the highest goal anyway.

The Judoka begins his massage by getting Leeda to relax. He does this by making use of both the effect of the massage itself and the effect of a light hypnotic trance induced by his suggestion and the monotonous rhythm of his voice. He wants the woman fully relaxed: i.e. not trying to do anything, not even to get into the attitude which it is the object of this massage to induce. He wants her free from obsession with anything. The Way itself can be an idol.

Then he begins to take her on what is called in current slang "a trip." The origin of this trip is the world of Leeda's ordinary reality. Its destination is the world of the true Judoka or true poet. Its object is to let her experience for a little while—and thereby get the feel of—the world of the person to whom life itself is a work of art, the person who can do judo or live the poetic way as a natural pressing out of his inner self. The trip, in short, is a way of cracking the young woman's cosmic egg.

Aldous Huxley explains in *The Doors of Perception* that it once seemed to him possible that "through hypnosis, for example, or autohypnosis, by means of systematic meditation, or else by taking the appropriate drug" he might be able so to change his ordinary mode of consciousness as to be able to know "from the inside" the world of Blake or Swedenborg or Bach. What happened to Huxley under the influence of mescalin was not exactly what he expected, yet in a way it accomplished that purpose.

The line of thinking behind Huxley's belief starts with Bergson's idea that the function of the brain and nervous system is in the main *eliminative* and not productive. We as human beings could sense great masses of material and potentially remember it all—we are all potentially Mind at Large—but if we did so we would be overwhelmed. To protect ourselves and to serve the functions of survival, we have learned to cut out much of what might be sense data to us; we have learned to *concentrate*. For survival purposes, this is very well. But a person pays a price for this necessary concentration: he becomes less alive than he might otherwise be. And if he stays too long and too exclusively in this world of reduced consciousness, perhaps especially in the verbal world of abstract language, his life becomes mere existence—and probably not even successful existence. The visionary, the poet, may be simply that man who has learned to be silent before the gods and thus to open a little the reducing valve. Another way to say this is that the visionary is he who has found the crack in his cosmic egg and has let flow through it what will.

By means of massage and hypnosis the Judoka takes Leeda on a trip from her ordinary "this world" of reduced awareness into the "other world" in which all is awareness and therefore love. It is an evolutionary trip, for it is precisely a journey into the maturity or full development of the human being—a maturity that includes, paradoxically and ironically, the wonder of the innocence of childhood. It is, of course, also a trip both to hell and to heaven.

Just as Leeda descended into a snake pit, she ascended beyond the estate of man, even fully mature man or woman, to the estate of the seer, the visionary, the mystic, the near-god. It seems likely, as Nietzsche suggests, that this is the direction of full humanity.

# LOVING

It is late afternoon. The day is balmy, and there is still a slight breeze off the water. The redhaired man walking along the beach toward the Judoka's enclosure is not much aware of any of these conditions; his mind is on other matters. Most prominent of the images holding his attention is that of the Judoka himself, although that of Leeda is also present, as is that of himself finally doing what he has to do against a shadowy background of prison cells and electric chairs. In the redhead's imagination the Judoka is dressed in a white judogi, although he has never seen the man dressed that way, and he is huge and terrible; nevertheless, he is now an object of prey.

Jealousy plays a part in the redhead's feelings about the Judoka. He is jealous of the man's possession of the woman and of the man's ability to draw people to him, even his enemies. Most of all he is jealous of the Judoka's apparent alliance with those forces that limit and smother other people. It is as if the monster has probed depths inaccessible to the redhead and emerged with strength beyond mortal due.

Hatred is mixed with fascination. The redhaired man has seen pictures of Geesink, the great Dutch world champion of judo, a man of immense stature in a white gi with his arms outstretched like wings. So the redhead sees the Judoka, hovering over the abyss that is his domain—everything and everybody. The redhead almost wishes to be swallowed up himself, but the thought of the nothingness is intolerable, like the white fog of the grave . . .

Now, on the hunting ground, the redhead's legs begin to hurt, and he has to push them to continue them on their appointed path. A small fear settles in the depths of his stomach, and he clamps it there and holds it, but it will not stay quite still, and the stomach begins to churn. On his brow a dull ache in the pattern of a frown starts on the outside and works its way into the interior. He knows, with fear, that these conditions will intensify until he is utterly insane. He will do anything at all to alleviate them.

When he arrives at the enclosure he finds the Judoka outside with the woman, both of them dressed in those hideous gis, warming up prior to a judo lesson. They see him, and he walks toward them, self-consciously and to his own dismay swaggering and smiling like a boy on the make and certain of conquest. But now he has committed himself, and his legs are strong again and the fear is gone and the churning and the aching have ceased. The swagger, like the ache before it, has moved inside.

At the edge of the marked square the redhead stops, still smiling, and pulls from his pocket a switchblade knife. "To even things up," he says. No more conversation is necessary, for in the meeting of their eyes the two men establish a channel of communication nearly as strong as that between Leeda and the Judoka. Even in this moment of crisis the Judoka reflects on how rare such rapport is—rare between man and woman, perhaps rarer still between man and man.

Leeda sees beyond the redhead's smile, which has now grown into a vile grin, and recognizes within him the despair that she felt in the depths of the massage. But the man does not quiver. He has passed the red stage of anger and hatred and gone into the black stage. His body and his face are cold and hard and cruel.

Yet curiously at that moment it is not the redhead who seems to Leeda the evil, the vast, foreboding shadow or beast; it is the Judoka. For the woman has learned her judo well, and she sees the scene through the eyes of the adversary. As the men begin to circle each other, the redhead with the knife lying lightly on his palm, the Judoka seems a giant in bleached off-white, his shoulders blown up out of proportion, his outspread arms like fins or wings, his movements catlike but vague. He is a threat and a foul thing to be eradicated. He is the object of a calm and quiet and bitter hatred.

The Judoka sees the scene as clearly as the redhead and the girl. Yet he is a spectator with a better viewpoint than either of them, and he sees that scene as an overlay of another: Inside himself is a fear like a bodily organ, fear of the redhaired man and the steel blade and the ultimate change. It is a balmy afternoon and a good day to die, but he fears dying nonetheless. The fear grows and he lets it grow, and it fills him and explodes and is gone, taking with it all expectation of life and concern with future or even present. And the Judoka himself feels a calmness and a coolness; he feels that he is a giant. He sees his opponent clearly and empathizes with him and anticipates through his own coolness a touch of warmth and pleasure. His mind vanishes.

Leeda has already been in the presence of two fights on this beach this summer and has thought that she has grown accustomed to the god of war, but now she knows that this familiarity was an illusion: when he hovers close, no human is ever really familiar with him. She is, however, now familiar enough with the idea of human contact in conflict to overcome its terror. She had come part of the way on the occasion of Tiny's attack, but she had not come far enough and she lost her self-control. Now she is quite calm and ready to help in an effective way. She waits only for an appropriate opening—one in which she can aid the Judoka without getting in his way. She is alert but not anxious, either to get in the fight or stay out of it; she feels very much as she did while dancing Leda.

The Judoka circles slowly, watching the whole man before him, conscious of every tensing of muscle in leg or arm, every flicker of the redhead's eye. The Judoka is a hunter seeking a weakness, but he is even more aware of being the hunted. Centering his awareness is the blade glinting in the late sun, at once fascinating him and repelling him, as a snake may do. The death that a moment ago he feared now appears almost as a consummation to be desired, a union with this knife and this man and all that is.

Lunging, the redhead plunges the knife at the Judoka's belly. The Judoka is aware, almost superficially aware, of sucking in and turning his stomach, thereby dodging it. At a more profound level he seems to have received the weapon into the space occupied by his body, taking it into him in a kind of joyous pain. He pulls the arm on into this space, aiding it, until the redhead's body crashes into his own. With this act the Judoka is for a moment maker, the architect of the situation. Suddenly he shifts from receiver to aggressor and smashes his fist not so much into as through the redhead's lower face. He follows the fist with an elbow.

An ordinary person would be felled by either blow, but the redhead is not ordinary now. He is protecting no self-image—all of that is burned out in his hatred—and he lets the blows go on through him, not even bothering to resist them, and thereby he is saved. He steps back.

The Judoka dives after him to take advantage of his stunned condition, but the redhead is now enjoying his role as recipient, as if being beaten were somehow the same pleasure as beating. He simply falls with the Judoka's dive, raising a foot almost playfully to offset only a little of its force—and the raised leg becomes a fulcrum over which the Judoka pivots and flies out onto the sand. The redhead is learning as he fights. The Judoka does a complete forward roll and stands again, but the redhead crowds him as he rises. The Judoka's arm, guarding his front, is pierced by the knife; both fighters feel the weapon enter the flesh, arousing in each a sensation that is at once pleasure and pain. Their eyes meet in a rapport closer than ever, and the Judoka knows that the redhead is driven to fight to victory or death. The Judoka pulls away and clasps his arm.

At this instant Leeda jumps forward with a blood-arousing Kiai! of which she has not before believed herself capable. It emerges with the frightening fierceness of the spit of a mother cat. The redhead turns in surprise and knows immediately that he cannot ignore this new adversary.

Leeda is fighting for the man she regards as her lover, yet her feelings now are curiously ambivalent. She thinks no words, for her mind is in the state of that of Takuan's swordsman; yet in that shadowy area beneath the intellect, between heart and brain as it seems, there are workings. She has been hurt by being left out of the communion between the two men. While she is perfectly clear about the identity of her adversary, there is a sense in which he is for her a representative of all men, including the Judoka. She is hostile, yet she desires communion with the redhead—jealously, perhaps, because the Judoka is in communion with him. And she has been denied this rapport because she is a woman. Fighting is not for women, men say, and for support of their contention point to their own heavier muscles. Granted, given equivalent attitudes, strength will tell; but attitudes are not always equivalent. The Judoka has told stories of little old men, eighty years of age, at the Kodokan, whom younger and stronger opponents cannot even touch. Men have strength, women a better natural and cultivated ability to yield.

The redhead and the woman circle. The redhead's confusion extends well into his conscious mind. Here he is, armed, fighting an unarmed woman! He dare not discard the knife, for there is no certainty that the man is permanently out of the fight; he holds the weapon but does not plan to use it. Still, that doesn't help much. His humiliation reaches crescendo level. He makes a grab at the woman, but she eludes him, grasps his arm, and pulls him forward and nearly off balance. He recovers.

To aggravate matters, here, even in this crisis, the redhead feels a lust for the woman. As the two people circle, they are not only adversaries, they are male and female. He recalls the feel of the knife against parting flesh. Dimly he is aware that his desire to possess and his desire to kill are not so very different.

Leeda is aware of it too, for she has now achieved the same rapport with this man that the Judoka has, perhaps even more. She realizes that one reason it is harder for a woman to fight a man than for a man to fight another man is that the duality of the situation is more likely to confuse the faces and figures of Mars and Venus.

The redhead charges her. She steps back, but in the rush he trips her. She falls. He straddles her. Briefly she feels a flash of delight wholly at variance with her intentions, but she quickly recovers. The redhead, uncertain now what to do, flips his knife to his left hand and slaps with his right. She dodges the blow, catches his hand and pulls it on, then squirms to the left and is free. She stands. The match is even again.

Leeda has more confidence now. She is more detached, and she grows playful; playful in the very face of possible, although perhaps accidental, death. While she is very clear in her regard of her adversary, he becomes even more strongly symbolic of the Judoka. Through two exchanges she sports with the man, giving full range to her desire to evade and her desire to yield. The battle is very even.

But Leeda is not quite a master, and she begins to weaken, to wish the conflict over. Her manner changes subtly, but the redhead is aware of it.

Meanwhile the Judoka has opened his jacket and completed wrapping his arm with his cloth belt. He watches Leeda with great pleasure; and for a moment his ego bloats with a great sense of achievement. Then he realizes, still with a smile, the absurdity of taking credit for what was already in his student from the start. Momentarily he is tempted to let the student go on with the battle, but he changes his mind for two reasons: Leeda may get badly injured; should she not, should she win, the redhead will know a crushing humiliation that may be even worse than death. Then he notices Leeda's weakening. He steps between the fighters.

Irrationally—and recognizing her own irrationality—Leeda hates him. He has interrupted an affair that brooks no interruption. Nevertheless, she steps back. She does not resent his assumption of generalship of the battle.

The redhead is disturbed by the change, for he knows that he himself is tiring and he supposes that the Judoka is now fresh. He shifts the position of his knife hand and prepares to throw. The circling movement begins again, but this time the redhead is intent in a new way: his harpoon and his lance are all the same—everything will ride on one act.

He throws. The Judoka dodges, hoping Leeda is not behind him. The momentary fear that she might be transforms itself into an intense and hard anger directed at the man who took the risk. All thought of being merciful leaves the Judoka. It is not only necessary but also desirable to kill this man who is driving desperately to his own death.

The two men close, but the man in the gi is now the obvious master of the situation. The redhead kicks at the Judoka's scrotum, but the Judoka deftly turns aside, grabs the foot, and flips the redhead onto his back. The redhead hits with a jar.

Before the redhead is wholly down, before he can raise a defensive foot or hand, the Judoka dives on him, his now loose white jacket flapping spread behind him so that he looks like a huge attacking bird. The blow of chest on chest is hard and sudden. The redhead tries to push away the alien brute with desperate but ineffective hands. As the redhead struggles, the Judoka merely shifts weight against strength, lying on his adversary like a sack of sand, relaxing, knowing a kind of terrible enjoyment.

Mingled in the Judoka are anger at this redhaired man, admiration for the fierceness and strength of the man's will, a touch of fear still remaining, and a sense of awe at what a human being steeled by will may become. He knows this redhead as he knows few people, and he knows that to let the man up may be only to force a replay that does not seem called for in the nature of things. He feels no sorrow and no pity: this is what the fates demand. He releases the neck, which he has been squeezing in the hard V of his arm, and raises his hand to chop across and into that neck and make a final consummation of the fight.

But now suddenly the redhead understands what everybody always knows but almost everybody leaves out of his habitual thinking. A shudder passes through his whole body as the recognition penetrates his inner being. Now he sees, and he cares and does not care, and he knows that power is a different kind of thing than he ever thought; and so knowing, he takes it on. He throws his head to the side and opens his neck to the Judoka's fatal chop.

And that very yielding stays the Judoka's hand. The Judoka, feeling the resignation and surrender all along his body, is frozen. His muscles lock; the game is over. A fighting redhead he could kill in a joyous paroxysm. This redhead he cannot attack at all.

Finally, the Judoka rises. He feels a desire to embrace in friendship his fallen adversary, but the intensity of his own animal or human savagery will not permit it, at least not for now, and he turns away with an indifference that is not at all holy. He takes the girl by the arm and walks down toward the waterline, never looking back.


The Judoka bathes his arm in the saltwater, and then, in the dusk, he and Leeda sit on the sand with the water periodically lapping at their bare feet. They talk in soft voices, and they sit side by side, but they are not really together. Both feel the separateness, and neither knows quite why it exists.

In the region of the Judoka's stomach there is a great, yawning hollowness. Separateness is both the glory and the pain of the human condition, but of the two the pain is the more intense sensation. The Judoka has just rejected a rapport of a size and kind that can yoke one person to another and thus both to all that exists; while he may accept others in the future—while he may possess one now with the person at his side—the loss of any one of these is real. In this case the rejection may have been inevitable. No man may have had within himself sufficient strength to reverse his emotional stance quickly and wholly enough to have made any difference. Yet it was the Judoka's own act. He built his own wall. And now he wonders if it is in his nature to build such walls, and if so, if he is even now building one against this woman at his side.

Leeda still feels a remnant of resentment against the Judoka for excluding her from a communion to which she had every right of access. She is angry with herself for feeling so, but the anger does not change the feeling. She senses the Judoka's hollowness and shares it, for she too knew the rapport and knows the loss, and she too was in her own way responsible. She senses also the wall, and in addition she is disappointed at the Judoka's human weakness, although she knows full well that she would be even more disconcerted if he had none.

As the dark increases the stars grow brighter. The Judoka recalls his first walk along the beach with this young woman. Then the time had not come to touch her; now the time has come and he is not whole. There is always something wrong, something incomplete! At times the Judoka has felt almost complete, and no doubt he has appeared that way and even appeared smug, yet he has always recognized that the completeness is illusory. And then he relaxes and settles back and looks at the stars and lets their brightness sweep through him. Of course he is incomplete; that is the human condition. Of course he has insufficient strength within himself; his weakness is in looking for it there. His very incompleteness is the pattern, and in recognizing it he is whole in the only kind of wholeness or holiness known to humankind. It is not a new discovery, but a renewed recognition of an old one.

He looks across at Leeda and sees that his communion with her is such that she has recovered with him. Or did she recover and share the recovery with him? It doesn't matter. He takes her hand and walks with her back to the enclosure.

There, he unknots her belt and slips her jacket from her shoulders.

"Aren't you being a bit forward with a concubine of the gods?" she asks, her eyes bright.

The Judoka grins, but he is beyond words for the present, as he is beyond concepts and meanings, like a haiku poet listening to the sound of rain. Then both the man and the woman know the full yielding that is the final fulfillment of the yielding way, the ultimate gentleness that is the giving over of self wholly to another person, that supreme poetry in which faith and hope come together as the same thing. It is a total yielding for both that is also for both a total possession.

Much later the Judoka finds words. "Isn't it written somewhere that we are to be as the gods?" he asks.

please visit
thejudoka.com

# W. D. NORWOOD, JR., WRITES ABOUT
# W. D. NORWOOD, JR.

Bill Norwood began his study of judo under John Daring at Texas Tech six years before the publication of this book. Norwood was a thirty-seven-year-old professor of English, and he had just read Eugen Herrigel's Zen in the Art of Archery. (He read it only because it was recommended by Charles Hardwick of the philosophy department, a man in whose judgment about books he had and has implicit confidence. At the time Norwood knew and cared nothing about Zen and still less about archery.) After he left Lubbock, he continued to practice judo from time to time and even to teach it informally, although he held, and still holds, only a brown belt. While teaching at the University of Southern Mississippi he published in The Southern Quarterly an article entitled "Judo as Poetic Way," and later expanded it into The Judoka. Norwood is now on the faculty of New College of California, an experimental school in Sausalito, where he is permitted to teach both literature and judo.

Mary Louise Norwood is perceptive in a number of areas in which her husband is not, and she is a careful and thoughtful reader; she served as a valuable critic both in pointing out weaknesses and in urging the retention of certain sections about which the author was doubtful. Tammye Norwood, a graceful young woman who is a far better natural athlete than her father, taught him a great deal simply by being; so did her younger brothers—Simmons, who can always lose himself in the moment, and Dub, who knows perhaps as well as anyone how to love. Much the same kind of thing could be said about Bill Norwood's parents, whom he at once emulates and reacts against, and his sister Nancy, who shares many of his own qualities in different forms. His brother-in-law, Dave Dumas, another philosophy professor, was enthusiastic about the article and thereby contributed to the writing of the book. The friend who was in all respects the chief influence on both the thought and style of the book was Lois Glenn. A student, Stephanie Taylor, read the first draft and gave a great deal of aid, especially in certain classroom discussions in which Norwood hammered out his ideas. Richard S. Johnson, who is now an editor of the Denver Post, was enthusiastic about the article and put Norwood in touch with his agent, Ruth Aley, a delightful person who sold the book almost at once to Knopf. At Knopf he fell into the hands of a young editor named Daniel Okrent, who made vast improvements on the book with a few well-considered suggestions.

(from 1973 Knopf edition)

# Writing as a Martial Art
by W. D. Norwood Jr. 1985

When we say that the pen is mightier than the sword, we mean that we can influence people more effectively by writing or talking to them than by fighting them. In this context writing is not a fighting art, it is something altogether different. In certain situations, however, it is very much a fighting art. For instance, we can think of the general writing up his battle plan for communication to his officers, or we can picture a MacArthur or a Charles de Gaulle formulating a proclamation to inspire his troops; too, we can remember governments using propaganda to further strategy and then providing misinformation to spies for the sake of tactical advantage. These instances are rather obvious. I mention them only to justify my treatment of writing as a fighting art.

My purpose here is to show that writing is a fighting art in a deeper and broader sense than the one reflected in the examples I've just given, then to show that much can be gained by studying and practicing it after the manner of the oriental martial artists. If I succeed, you will see—better than most people ever see—why universities put great emphasis on writing courses, and you will see also why I want you to read *The Judoka*.

Everyone realizes that writing is a way of communicating with other people. What many people fail to realize is that it is also a way of communicating with oneself. In other words, it is a way of thinking. The general writing out his battle order is developing and refining it as well as preparing it for distribution; he is thinking through it, seeing potential weaknesses and opportunities, perhaps revising it. Because his writing is in essence a thinking process that may affect the substance as well as the form of his plan, I say that writing is a fighting art in a deeper sense than a person might first think. Because writing may be a factor in coping with all sorts of problems—not just military ones—I say that it is a fighting art in a broader sense than the term implies if taken as strictly literal.

Thinking is largely a matter of manipulating symbols, and most of the symbols we use are words. Reasoning is for the most part relating sentences in order to discover and justify new sentences that seem to follow from them in legitimate ways. Imagining may be simple refitting of sensed properties—as when we put green from the grass together with roundness and intensity from the sun to make a green sun—but most of our imagining is complex realigning of abstractions that "exist" chiefly as words. Since reasoning and imagining are the major constituents of thinking, the core process of thinking is the choosing and ordering of words. Writing is fundamentally the same thing: a process of choosing and ordering words.

Speaking also is a process of selecting and arranging words, but the speaker can use voice and gesture to help him get across his meaning. The writer has to use punctuation marks to substitute for voice and gesture, and punctuation marks are essentially just words (in a special alphabet) that indicates silences or subtle modifications of sound. The writer, therefore, has to be more precise in his choosing and ordering of words than the speaker does, and his writing serves better than talking to train in the core process of thinking. Students should study speech as well as writing, but discussion of that matter is outside my present scope. My point here is that a student should learn to write well for the sake of his ability to think as well as his ability to communicate with other people.

I must add here that writing is of importance not only in preparing a person to think but in helping him conduct the actual process of thinking. If you watch carefully in restaurants, you often see somebody, perhaps sitting over a cup of coffee, "figuring something out" by making notes on a paper napkin or a legal pad. In some cases, of course, the person is "figuring" in the literal sense of doing arithmetic or even algebra or calculus; but in other cases he is writing words. The person we see in the restaurant is not likely to have a formal theory like mine that relates writing and thinking; he just knows by experience that he thinks better when he writes things down than he does when he tries to do everything "in his head." We, however, can analyze the situation and see how his notes help him. First, they function as a memory device: having written down his ideas, he doesn't forget them, nor does he have to divert any of his attention to holding them in his mind. Second, they force him to clarify what seems clear enough "in the head" but is found to be far too vague to state accurately on paper. Third, they enable him to see, literally, what he is saying and thereby to observe strengths and weaknesses of his position not apparent in the airy milieu of pure mind.

The average person who makes notes in a restaurant probably does no more than make random notes, so he gets nothing like as much help in cultivating his thought as he would get by writing out a full and coherent discourse. If his problem is a minor one or a routine one, he probably doesn't need to go to the trouble of writing out a full discourse; but an educated person should realize that he could work in this way to advantage in coping with a major problem.

Selecting and arranging words is a complex and subtle art. A person makes mistakes in writing the same way he makes them in mathematics—by picking the wrong symbols and putting them in the wrong places; the results of poor writing are the same as those of poor mathematics-wrong answers. The person who wants to get right answers has to master the art of writing, and he masters it in roughly the same way he masters any other art.

One valuable approach to the mastery of an art, while not exactly unique to the oriental martial arts, is perhaps most easily understood through them. It's an approach that hasn't been used (so far as I know) by any developing writer, but it's one that I think might be used to great advantage.

When a streetfighter strikes or kicks or chokes or breaks free or makes any other combative movement, his concern is exclusively for the external effect of his action: for the effect, in other words, on his adversary. The serious martial artist is as concerned as the streetfighter with the external effect, but is equally concerned with the internal effect of his movement: that is, with the effect on his own body, mind, and spirit. This split vision is the chief factor, I think, in making the martial artist an exceptionally able fighting man. It has a by-product effect of making him also a moral man and, in many cases, a rather good thinker.

Split vision affects the martial artist internally in several ways. Importantly, it tends to produce harmony between mind and body and among the muscles, and that harmony makes for power and grace. Perhaps even more importantly, the split vision sets attitude, by which I mean posture both literal and figurative. The combination of harmony and attitude enables the person to get into the right rhythm for his activity; and rhythm, of course, is one of the primary keys to effective performance in any art.

By reading *The Judoka* you can learn a little about the split vision and the attitude, both of which are as appropriate to writing as they are to any other kind of activity. Then, by making an effort, you can to some degree adapt the split vision to the writing process, and you can certainly adopt the attitude If you do so, you will be treating writing as a martial art, and I think you will get results comparable to those the martial artist gets in hand-to-hand combat. Schopenhauer says that what a man writes in order to understand a subject himself is more likely to be worth reading than what he writes for the sake of helping other people understand the subject.

When I wrote *The Judoka* I wasn't thinking much about applications to the art of writing. I wrote it to serve as a sort of casual textbook for some judo classes I was teaching. But I had a secondary purpose that came to be as important to me as the primary one: I wanted to show that the "judo principle"—push when the adversary pulls, pull when he pushes—can be usefully employed in dealing with many kinds of problems in addition to those of hand-to-hand combat. The idea, stated differently, is that a wide variety of problems can be solved by making use of the very forces that are causing them. To illustrate the idea, I can refer to Churchill and Roosevelt in the Lend Lease deal, or to Kennedy "turning" the religious issue in the 1960 election; all three of those men were using the judo principle, although so far as I know none of them had any acquaintance with martial art.

I had occasion to use the principle myself in writing the book. I thought I was writing about judo, but I couldn't seem to package all I wanted to say in any well-ordered form. I found myself continually trying to write not about judo but about a man who practices judo. Finally, 1 gave up and started describing that man and then commenting on that description. Suddenly, I had an organization that worked.

In this paper I have described writing as a "martial art" in that it is a problem-solving art. Too, I have suggested practicing it in the spirit and posture of a martial artist, and I have urged you to read *The Judoka* in order to learn to practice it in that manner. Now I suggest that in reading the book you pay special attention to its treatment of problem solving, for I think that the judo principle can help you smooth out your writing and at the same time add to its strength as a means of coping with many kinds of external problems.

W. D. Norwood Jr. — A Brief Biography

W.D. (Bill) Norwood, Jr., was born in Paris, Texas in 1929 at the beginning of the Great Depression, and raised in the small Southeast Texas town of Beaumont during the peak of the Texas oil boom which started just a few miles away at the Spindletop Ranch. His father was the proprietor of a small but successful office supply store, the Beaumont Typewriter and Supply Company, and his mother was a schoolteacher. Raised in the Southern Baptist Church, Norwood entered Baylor University at age sixteen to study English literature and theology with the intention of preparing for the ministry. After graduation, with the U.S. engaged in military conflict on the Korean Peninsula, he delayed entering seminary in order to enlist in the United States Navy. While in route to fight in that conflict as a Communications Officer aboard the Naval Destroyer U.S.S. Brinkley Bass, the Korean Armistice Agreement was signed, effectively ending active hostilities, and the Brinkley Bass was diverted to Tokyo, Japan. His time in Japan was to greatly alter the course of his life, providing as it did his first sustained exposure to the cultural traditions of the Far East. He later attended naval flight school in San Diego, California, prior to honorable discharge at the rank of Lieutenant.

Following his discharge from the Navy, Norwood entered seminary in Berkeley, California, but soon discovered that his theological beliefs were evolving and, being unwilling to tie his livelihood to a particular set of beliefs, he dropped out of seminary and returned to Beaumont, Texas. While working for his father as a typewriter repairman, he married and began study for a Master's Degree in English literature at Lamar University with the financial aid of the G.I. Bill. After completing a Ph.D. in English literature at the University of Texas at Austin, he would go on to teach and pursue scholarly research at Southwest Texas State University, Texas Tech University, Angelo State University, and the University of Southern Mississippi as he advanced through the academic ranks. He founded the renowned Center for Writers during his time at University of Southern Mississippi in Hattiesburg.

In the early 1970s, while Chair of English at the University of Southern Mississippi, Dr. Norwood emerged as an outspoken opponent of the university's effort to resist racial integration, and his stance on this issue led to his separation from the university (for a book-length account of this dark period in the history of the university, and Norwood's role in the controversies that ensued, see Exit 13: Oppression and Racism in Academia (1982), by Monte Piliawsky). During an extended legal battle with the University of Southern Mississippi that centered on the issue of academic freedom, Dr. Norwood was briefly Dean of Humanities at New College of California, in San Francisco, but soon after left academia, moved to Houston, Texas, and opened a small business. For the next nine years, Dr. Norwood was the proprietor of Norwood Stationers, later the Norwood Office Products Company, before gradually returning to the activity he enjoyed the most, teaching. At the time of his death, in 1998, Dr. Norwood taught English literature at Tomball College, outside of Houston, Texas. Prior to joining the Tomball faculty, he had taught as an adjunct there, as well as at the University of Houston, Prairie View A & M, and Houston Baptist University.

Early in his career, while teaching at San Angelo State University, a routine traffic stop would lead to a life-long friendship with then San Angelo Police Sargent John Daring, a judoka who taught the fighting art in his spare time. This chance encounter began his study of Judo, an interest that would continue to occupy him throughout his life. At the time of his death he was revising a work entitled Laffite's Ghost[1] exploring the idea of moral piracy, with courage, love, and a certain degree of justifiable rapaciousness as central to his image of a full life.

1. MWI publishing will be relaeasing this title in the second half of 2015.

To purchase high quality prints
of the cover artwork
by
Michael Nolan
please visit
www.thejudoka.com

# MWI Publishing
# do you have

stories to tell

poems to share

information to impart

*together we will make it happen*

www.mwipublishing.com